Dream
Weaving

Dream Weaving

Using Dream Guidance to Create Life's Tapestry

Emily L. VanLaeys

ARE
PRESS

ASSOCIATION FOR
RESEARCH AND
ENLIGHTENMENT

A.R.E. Press   •   Virginia Beach   •   Virginia

A.R.E. Press
215 67th Street
Virginia Beach, VA 23451-2061

Library of Congress Cataloging-in-Publication Data

VanLaeys, Emily L.
  Dream weaving : using dream guidance to create life's tapestry / Emily L. VanLaeys.
     p. cm.
Includes bibliographical references.
  ISBN 0-87604-471-2
  1. Dreams--Religious aspects--Christianity. 2. Spiritual life--Christianity. I. Title.
  BR115.D74 V36 2001
  154.6'3--dc21

                                                              00-011583

Cover and interior design by Lightbourne

To my husband, Mark, and my children, Vera and Peter, the main characters in many of my dreams and most of my life stories.

ACKNOWLEDGMENTS

I would like to thank my parents, Mary and Gene Lissandrello, for instilling in me a love of the written word. I am also indebted to Professor Eugene Bar, who taught me to pay attention to my dreams in Philosophy 140 at William Smith College in 1975. A special thanks to A. Robert Smith, editor of *Venture Inward* magazine, whose encouragement kept me writing while all the other editors were saying, "Sorry. No room!"

I also appreciate the insights and suggestions of my friends, Anna Siudy, Jan Novak, and Kate Evjen Whittaker, as this book was in process. And I am grateful to Evelyn Skellie, who let me print the manuscript on her printer when mine malfunctioned!

How fortunate I am to have a warm, helpful editor in Brenda English. Thanks, Brenda, especially for the subtitle suggestion! I also would like to thank Norine Conroy, editor of *Grace: A Companion for Women on Their Spiritual Journey*, who first published the chapter "To Find the Soul in Housework" in the September/October 1999 issue of her magazine.

Finally, my deepest thanks go to the three loves of my life: Mark, Vera, and Peter, without whom this book would not exist.

CONTENTS

PREFACE

In 1992, when my desire to write had been set at "slow simmer" for seven years, since the birth of my first child, I dreamed that I was visiting a college campus. Finding myself alone, without the usual family obligations, I thought about going to my room to write. But what about? No ideas came, and I decided I would much rather relax with a good book. I headed for the college library, hoping to find a novel with a spiritual message.

The library contained vast rooms, impressive with their stone walls and leather chairs. As I wandered from room to room, a book appeared in my hands. I didn't even look at it because I hadn't come to the fiction section yet, and I wanted a novel. When I had passed through several rooms without finding any fiction, I glanced down at the book I was holding. It was about dream interpretation. I thought: "This is definitely something I want to read, but I still want a novel."

At the time, I had no idea what this dream meant, but I recorded it in my dream journal because the mysterious book in my hands begged to be noticed. Six years later, while reviewing my journals for this book, *Dream Weaving*, I rediscovered the library dream and realized that the book in my hands was this one—the book I would create when my desire to write had increased from a slow simmer to a rolling boil. This is not, however, a book on dream interpretation. For people who seek understanding about the meaning of dreams in general and their own in particular, that type of book can be found in abundant supply in bookstores and libraries. *Dream Weaving: Using Dream Guidance to Create Life's Tapestry* is a spiritual memoir in which I trace my journey from that "wild spring age" when practical goals were something to scoff at, to a middle-aged delight in the purpose and meaning of an ordinary life. This path is illumined by the light that has been revealed to me as I ponder my dreams and weave their messages into the fabric of my everyday experiences.

My dream visit to the college library, a symbol of knowledge and learning, came at a time when I was preoccupied with my duties as the mother of young children, and as a church and community volunteer. When I had some free moments for literary diversion, I just wanted to curl up with a good book. Writing anything myself required too much energy and concentration. But the source of wisdom I've come to call the Dream Weaver knew that the time was coming when I would want to return to the "hallowed halls of learning," to discover what spiritual wisdom I could glean from my life and dreams, and weave these thoughts together to share with others.

Who is the Dream Weaver who lives in each of us and who delivers nocturnal messages full of strange and mysterious images? Dream books offer many theories: scientific, psychological, and spiritual. It is up to each dreamer to decide what is the source of these fascinating, bizarre, and often frightening nighttime tales. My dreams seem to come from different sources: some from my subconscious, some from my higher self, and others from a divine messenger—an angel, spirit guide . . . God?

Out of the many dream guidance books currently available, I have used only two to aid in the interpretation of my dreams: *Dreams—Your Magic Mirror: With Interpretations of Edgar Cayce* by Elsie Sechrist and *The Encyclopedia of Dreams: Symbols and Interpretations* by Rosemary Ellen Guiley. I used these guides to determine the meanings of universal symbols, but I relied on my own intuition and imagination to relate my dreams to my life experiences. After all, the true meaning of any dream is an elusive mystery. I never know for certain when I have unearthed the "right" meaning or guidance from a dream, but the more pieces of the puzzle that fit together, the more confident I feel about the correctness of my interpretation. If one of the symbolic meanings found in these books corresponds to a current issue or ongoing theme in my life—and especially if I've had more than one dream containing similar symbolism—I tend to think that the Dream Weaver has gotten through to me.

Dream interpretation books offer numerous instructions for recall and retention: "Keep a pad by your bed and record your dreams as soon as you wake up. Write down every single dream. Each one provides the key to an important issue in your life." Since I frequently awake in the middle of the night and often remember more than one dream, I would be perpetually tired if I followed this advice. I think a good night's sleep is more important than most of my dreams. But when I have one that is particularly vivid, or full of fascinating imagery, or one in which the Dream Weaver speaks to me in audible words laden with meaning, I pay attention.

When I read a self-help book of any kind, I tend to extract those lessons that appear valuable and leave the rest for those who gain the most by following a set of instructions letter by letter. My method of recording only the dreams that make some impact on my conscious mind prevents me from growing discouraged and giving up the practice altogether. Each dreamer should experiment with different ways of working with dreams to discover one that is user-friendly.

One technique for procuring dream guidance, which I learned about from my reading, is to pray for insight about a particular problem before going to sleep. There have been times when I've requested guidance at night and awoke the next day, complaining: "Hey, where's my answer?" But this method has frequently worked for me, and I have included several of these "dream questions and answers" in my book. Just because something doesn't always work, doesn't mean it won't work very well at other times. When the Dream Weaver has something to say, she will!

Is it important to remember our dreams at all? Why bother, we think, when we are existing on the surface of life, dashing from one activity to another: office, school, shopping, meetings. Who has time to stop and reflect on the "why" of it all? But when we do manage to slow down, to dig for the deeper meanings of life, we may find that our dreams open new vistas on some of these mysteries.

The importance of dreams is frequently referred to by Edgar Cayce (1877-1945), who is considered the most reliable and best-documented psychic of the twentieth century. Over a period of forty years, Cayce gave more than 14,000 "readings" to thousands of individuals in response to questions about physical ailments, philosophical concerns, and spiritual needs. Many of these readings referred to dreams, such as, reading 5754-3[1]: " . . . such experiences as dreams, visions and the like, are but the *activities* in the unseen world of the real self of an entity." If the strange goings on of our dreams are actually taking place in the unseen world, it definitely behooves us to pay attention to them!

Another of Cayce's readings on the importance of dreams is 294-15: "As we see, all visions and dreams are given for the benefit of the individual, [if they would] but interpret them correctly, for we find that visions, or dreams, in whatever character they may come, are the reflection, either of the physical condition . . . or of the subconscious . . . or a projection from the spiritual forces to the subconscious of the individual . . . "

Author Madeleine L'Engle offers still another reason

for paying attention to our dreams: "All forms of art are consciousness expanders . . . And so are our dreams. I want to remember them . . . so that I will be less insular, less afraid to travel in foreign lands. We are very foolish if we shrug and patronizingly consider that these voyages are not real."[2]

In writing this book, I realized that some of my dreams *are* art forms in themselves. Working with them has expanded my consciousness and helped me to discover mountains of creativity in the landscape of my subconscious. I have unearthed inner strengths by facing the "bogeymen" of my nightmares, and I have learned to be more comfortable traveling in the "foreign lands" which I call the Dream Weaver's world. I hope that some of my voyages will encourage readers to do the same.

---

1. The Edgar Cayce readings are organized by a numbering system in which, for example, 5754-3 indicates a reading for the person assigned number 5754 and is the third reading for that person.
2. L'Engle, Madeleine, *A Circle of Quiet*. Farrar, Straus and Giroux, New York, N.Y., 1972, pp. 225-226.

1

When Life Has Other Plans
Empty Paper Bags and a Cozy Cabin

*O*ne ordinary night, cold and clear, I hauled a load of books to the campus library and glanced skyward to behold a large, glowing orb drifting toward me. It must be the flying saucer I'd been looking for since childhood, I thought, the one that carried beings of beauty and wisdom, far surpassing that of anyone I knew on earth, who would welcome me into their midst and teach me the secrets of the universe as we sped, faster than light, toward an exotic planet orbiting some distant star—in the Pleiades, perhaps. There would be no suffering on that planet and no mundanities. Life there would be full of adventure, romance, and wonders I couldn't imagine. The celestial body drew closer until I could see its blazing announcement: "Bank with Geneva Savings & Loan." I trudged on toward the library to research ideas for one of my anomalous courses, possibly my independent study in children's fantasy literature or the bidisciplinary English-physics course on time. (*Will* there be an end to time, when all things become one with the Eternal Now, without beginning or end?)

For much of the early part of my life, when I had not yet learned to appreciate the mysteries of everyday life and nocturnal dreams, I dwelt frequently in the imaginary spaces in my mind. In my childhood bed, I fantasized that a fairy came through my window to take me for a midnight flight to a heavenly ball where I'd be dressed in satin to dance with the fairy prince. I cried to God in my prayers because I knew the magic in my books existed just beyond the veil that He drew aside for a privileged few. When I sat in my pew at church, the minister's voice was a soothing hum in the background of my reverie. I was sure the entire building was being lifted into the clouds by the hand of God, and no one else knew it because the stained-glass windows obscured the view.

In my teen years, I let go my dreams of magical excursions and galactic voyages, but other ideals and visions steered me clear of the path that might have led to an earlier contentment with everyday life. My memory of the prince I'd danced with among the stars clouded my vision, so the boys I knew, with their pimples and wisecracks, all blurred before my eyes. The few whom I imagined could be as handsome and exciting as my fantasy were wise enough to avoid my crystal-crusted gaze.

Equally romantic about my future career options, I spurned my high school guidance counselor's suggestion that I pursue a teaching profession. Teachers merely conveyed to a new generation the same knowledge that had been imparted to them in their youth. They were spokes in the wheel of ordinary life, ensuring the repetition of ideas and disciplines from one decade to the next. My goal was more grandiose: to break out of the wheel of life and into the realm of spirit and imagination. I would be an author and wow the world with my astounding ideas!

In college, I chose to major in English, because literature was the field that captured my imagination and was, I thought, the logical foundation for a writing career. There were very few required courses at William Smith College in the post-rebellion seventies. Between literature classes, I dipped into history and psychology, dabbled in art, and dallied with religion and philosophy.

In my senior year, a philosophy professor taught us to record our dreams and interpret them according to the methods of Carl Jung. One of my dreams placed me in a family that had lost all of its material wealth, except for a station wagon that would take us on a camping trip through Vermont. The mother gave each of us, her children, some empty paper bags to sell for forty cents apiece. We were to tell prospective customers that the bags contained surprises. I was appalled by this deceitfulness, but I went with this family, and we sold the bags. At the end of the dream, we were sitting in a cozy cabin with a crowd of happy people, singing camp songs.

This dream journey appeared to symbolize my going out into the work world without money or experience. I would have to sell myself to a prospective employer, and my ability to write an A+ paper on a book I didn't understand was not going to impress anyone in the business world. I knew I couldn't support myself on the hope of becoming an author "someday." But there was a surprise in those empty bags, something known only to my higher self, the part of me that was connected to the divine Weaver of Dreams. That surprise would open the way to a future, not of monumental success or extraordinary adventure, but one in which I would know satisfaction and delight in a simple home life, where the Divine Mystery reveals itself through family and friends, meditation and prayers, nature and dreams, my everyday tasks and my imagination.

After several months of job hunting, the first empty bag was sold to a business school in Washington, D.C., where I was hired as assistant to the placement director. For nine months, I sat at my desk, answering the phone, typing letters, and processing forms for students and alumni seeking work in an arena beyond my ken. How would I make my way into that glorious realm of adventure and creativity when I felt like the miller's daughter, imprisoned in a turret spinning room with heaps of straw around me? Since no little man came to turn the straw into gold, I looked for other ways to escape that stifling environment. I took a night class in creative writing and enrolled in the Rosicrucian correspondence course in order to learn the "Secret Method for the Mastery of Life." I dated a Japanese man whose fast car and smoking habit I would not have tolerated if I hadn't been so desperate for excitement. After all, it *was* Manabu's car that took me to my writing class, night-clubs, and restaurants, when I would have stayed home alone for fear of the dark city streets.

When his work permit expired in December, Manabu returned to Japan, and I released simultaneous sighs of relief and loss, and then reassessed my predicament. I had sent applications to several graduate English programs, and I was interviewing for "more interesting" jobs during my lunch hour. The Peace Corps was in need of French-speaking volunteers to teach English in Africa, so I signed up for a Saturday French class. Some knowledge of French might help me to get into graduate school, if not the Peace Corps, I reasoned.

When none of the interviews resulted in a new job and several Ph.D. programs had rejected me on the grounds that undergraduate courses such as *"Studies in Embarrassed Art"* and *"Man in Space"* could not have prepared me for the rigors of postgraduate academia, I received a letter from an old friend, inviting me to join her in the Rockies of Montana and pan for gold at the Big Sky employment agency. Here was a chance for adventure, not quite as exotic as Africa, but not requiring knowledge of a foreign language, so I responded to my friend and to the universe with a loud and hopeful "Yes!"

So many of our life decisions are based on circum-stances: the doors that are closed to us, past choices which have created "made beds" that we must now lie in, and the opportunities that call us out of those beds, which, however undesirable, may comfort us with their familiarity. I never would have considered a move to Montana if I hadn't been trapped between an unbearable situation and what appeared to be the only opening between my turret window bars that was large enough for me to squeak through.

Later, when a plethora of angel books appeared on bookstore shelves, I concluded that my guiding spirits had manipulated the events that led to the decision that would eventually culminate in the fulfillment of my "empty bag" dream about a contented life in a cozy home. While my body was being transported through time and space, by train and plane, to be delivered at the feet of those majestic, soaring mountains, my soul was singing and dancing with my heavenly helpers in that timeless realm where the destiny of each spirit is known. Of course, I was ignorant of all the commotion in the unseen world, where angels slapped each other on the back and toasted my higher self with glasses of sparkling holy water.

When I arrived in Whitefish, the charming mountain town I had envisioned, I discovered that my friend had decided to enter the state university in Bozeman, 250 miles to the southeast, and it would be my privilege to help her move! Bozeman was a flat, sprawling city, with the mountains I had come to venerate looming aloof and silent on the distant horizon. This was not what I'd had in mind when I began my adventure, but an advertisement in the "Help Wanted" section of the newspaper hinted at exciting possibilities with the Yellowstone Park Company in Wyoming. I apologized to my friend for deserting her so soon after my arrival, but Bozeman couldn't hold me. She seemed to understand, and now I wonder if she felt the presence of unseen helpers as they guided me onto the bus that would take me to the Mammoth Hot Springs

Hotel eighty miles away in Yellowstone National Park.

I went there for a refreshing interlude between the "First Job" chapter of my life and "Buckling Down to My True Purpose," never guessing that the angels had already entitled it: "True Love, True Purpose." As a daughter of the women's liberation movement, I knew the importance of establishing myself in a career before I could hope to enter into a "marriage of equality." I remember saying to my mother, while we were hanging clothes together one summer between college terms, "I won't marry any man who isn't willing to share all of the household chores." Mom had replied, "You can't plan ahead when it comes to marriage." Well, just because she didn't, doesn't mean I can't, I assured myself. I might have been fuzzy about the career I was going to embark on, but I knew what I wanted in a marriage, and I didn't want it at all for several more years.

That summer in Yellowstone, I wasn't even looking for romance. In college, I had traded my fantasy prince for the more mature philosophy that lasting love must begin as a slow-simmering friendship and increase in flavor gradually, as shared experiences are stirred into the pot. I had experimented with two such friendly transformations. The first time, it was two years before we were ready for the taste test. Things were hot and spicy by then. He burned his tongue and backed off, leaving me alone with a half-empty pot. The second friend filled the pot with marshmallows. Soft and sweet, but lacking sustenance, that relationship gradually evaporated, clean and easy. I wouldn't have time for that kind of experiment during my Yellowstone stopover.

I sold my second empty paper bag to the tour bus dispatch office, where my duties closely paralleled the "straw-spinning" chores I'd left hundreds of miles away. But here, the scene outside my window featured a forested mountain instead of brick buildings, and when I went to lunch at the staff cafeteria, I found myself watching a certain captivating young man. Tall and lanky, with a thick mop of fire-red hair, he sported a shrubby moustache that lent an air of maturity to his impish grin. I felt the warmth of that grin once, when he happened to sit across the table from me during lunch. But usually he was surrounded by pretty waitresses, or else I didn't see him at all. Better not to think about him anyway, I told myself. I had just been accepted to a master's program in women's literature at Goddard/Cambridge Graduate School, where I would enroll in the fall, and I would never see him again.

Little did we know, but our guardian angels were scheming together, making certain that we didn't let this carefully planned opportunity pass us by. So it happened that I took a bus tour of the park by myself one Sunday, and lunchtime found me at the Old Faithful Inn, where I saw him sitting at a table in the cafeteria as soon as I walked in. He was alone, too, a fact that gave me courage to take my tray to his table and set it down across from him.

"Hi, my name is Emily. I work at Mammoth. Haven't I seen you there?" I asked innocently.

"Yes, I'm the bartender at the Mammoth Hotel. My name's Mark. Aren't you Jim Garvey's girlfriend?"

"No, I don't even know Jim Garvey." So much for romantic beginnings. Mark never did remember seeing me prior to that day. He likes to tell people how we first met at Old Faithful, fifty miles from where we lived. And I like to think of the geyser as a metaphor for our relationship, Old Faithful being neither the largest nor highest geyser in Yellowstone, yet it is known the world over for its remarkable constancy. Unlike most of the thermal features in Yellowstone Park, the heights, intervals, and length of Old Faithful's play have changed very little since its discovery in 1870. Just so, the fountain of love which began bubbling between us that day has not reached extraordinary heights, nor has it enveloped us in its tender mist on a predictable basis. But our mutual care and nurture of this fountain ensures a consistent display of love that never ceases to bubble altogether.

On our first date, Mark's Chevy pickup hauled us up a rugged mountain to Jardine, a deserted mining village at the park's north entrance. Halfway up, we stopped to visit another Yellowstone employee who lived with her husband and small son in a log cabin near a wild, rushing stream. She invited us in for a tour of their home: stoneware plates on the kitchen hutch, a wood stove in the living room, a patchwork quilt on the bed, and mountains, water, and trees framed by calico curtains.

What could be more idyllic? To live in a place like this with a husband like Mark! The thought slipped out before I could stifle it. How could I be thinking about marriage with a man I had only just met? Well, I did mean someone *like* Mark. In a home like this one. It was a lot like the Vermont cabin in the dream I had forgotten, but my soul's longing for that kind of homey warmth begged to be heard above all my egotistical striving for grandeur.

I had sold the paper bags in my dream for forty cents apiece. In dreams and biblical stories, forty days or forty years is a period of spiritual incubation, trial, and initiation. Money denotes one's feelings of self-worth and self-esteem. Selling empty paper bags certainly implies a lack of self-worth, but the symbolism of "forty" suggests that the wonderful surprise would be revealed after I completed my spiritual trial and initiation. When that occurred, I would discover that my soul's desire was not at all what *I* thought a happy life entailed.

Farther up on the mountain's ridge, Mark and I wandered around the miners' cemetery, reading the weathered tombstones that were engraved with mountain scenes and horses. One had been carved to look like a tree stump with a scroll bearing the name of a person who was no longer. The scene was set for a discourse on otherworldly realms. As the sun descended and sent explosions of peach and strawberry above the distant mountains, we exchanged speculations about an afterlife existence.

Several horses grazed in a field bordering the cemetery. Mark held a clump of long grass over the fence top and called softly to them so that we could stroke their velvety muzzles as we talked. We barely knew each other, and yet we were delving into a subject my college boyfriends wouldn't touch. When I had dipped my cup of curiosity below the surface of life, they had grown uneasy. Mark knew a lot more about the mountain wilderness than he did about ethereal planes, but his eager spirit was ripe for explorations of all kinds. That night marked the beginning of a joint quest for love and spiritual wisdom that would carry us over more mountains and valleys than we traveled in our two months together in Yellowstone Park.

I forgot all about the warning to myself: not to get involved with someone from whom I would have to part. When we were together, our spirits danced in that timeless realm where everything is as it should be and every thought is of the golden *now*. But our bodies remained on the earth plane, and so the time came to speak of the future and practicalities. Mark's family lived in New Jersey, but his heart belonged to the craggy Rockies and the wild spaces in between. His plan was to travel around Montana with his biology degree and investigate different types of hospital work. He invited me to join him, but I couldn't picture myself living in the back of a pickup truck, destination unknown. No, the summer idyll would have to end. I would go east to graduate school as intended, and we would continue on our separate, lonely paths.

That was the practical plan, but when it came time to part at the Bozeman airport, we realized that a bond had been forged between us, too strong to be broken by time or space or individual goals. "We'll be together again, soon," Mark promised before I boarded the plane. And so we were.

2

Building an Ideal
The City of Peace

*M*ark and I had known each other nine months when we were married in a simple ceremony at my mother's church. He had completed his first two weeks working as a medical technologist for a Boston hospital. I was writing my master's thesis on nineteenth-century women writers while looking for a student teaching position in a Boston school. (One teacher told me, "Literature is for the leisure classes," and another said he taught his students to read the newspaper and critique television commercials, so I decided that teaching English would not be my vocation.) Our one-bedroom apartment was furnished with my parents' old kitchen table, a castoff sofa and chair from Mark's brother, and a double mattress and boxsprings that we purchased with our wedding gift money. We began our life voyage together, and so our goals and accomplishments would be the result of shared decisions.

Much of our first year as a couple was spent learning that we could love each other in spite of the many disagreements that kept cropping up as two imperfect people attempted to twine their separate needs and desires into a single strong cord. Just before our first anniversary, I had a dream that reminded me of the spaceship I had once hoped would take me away from the mundane world, which, after all, is central to the settled, married life. In this dream, I was an alien visiting earth, or else I was an earthling visiting another planet. I had to go through customs before I would be allowed into this other world. A barrier came down in front of me, and a man behind it looked out from a window and asked for some identification. I noticed a water fountain and tried to drink from it, but I couldn't figure out how it worked. I decided it was a test to see whether or not I belonged in that world.

Somehow, I managed to get past the wall into the new world, but I had to return because Mark was waiting for me on the customs side, and some things had spilled out of my pocketbook there. Either Mark or the man in the window told me that my goal in that world was to achieve peace, love, truth, and beauty. I answered that even though they sounded trite, those abstract ideas really did express my goals. Then Mark asked me what my immediate, concrete objective was. I replied, "I want to found my own city where truth, peace, love, and beauty will reign."

All that time, I was picking up the items that had fallen out of my purse. Mark asked why I was wasting my time with such trivial things. I told him that, even though they were very little, each item was a part of my life and was meaningful to me.

I believe that my desire to cross over from one world into another one can be interpreted on two levels: One was the need for transition from the "honeymoon" period of my relationship with Mark into a more mature period of cooperation and commitment; the second was my longing for transformation from this material existence to a higher spiritual level. I did not make any attempt to interpret this dream when it came to me in 1978. When we had been married for twenty years, and Mark gave me a topaz ring to compensate for the engagement ring I never had, I understood that the two goals for an enduring partnership and for spiritual enlightenment can be achieved concurrently when two people tread the path of life together.

At the time this dream came to me, I had not yet read the wisdom of Edgar Cayce, the modern-day psychic and prophet who advised us to set spiritual ideals that will aid us in making our life decisions. One special group of readings, the 262 series, became the basis for *A Search for God, Books I and II,* still used today by study groups of the Cayce material. Chapter 3, Book I, discusses ideals and what they are: "An ideal is something beyond and above us toward which we build. . . . The true ideal is the highest spiritual attainment to be reached on this material plane; hence, it follows that our ideal must be found in Christ, who is the Way."

This need for a spiritual ideal was not something I was consciously aware of in my early adult life, but seeing this dream recorded in my journal twenty years ago confirms that my inner self, my soul, was very aware of its importance. The water fountain evokes the image in Revelation 21:6: "I am Alpha and Omega, the beginning and the end. I will give unto him that is athirst of the fountain of the water of life freely." The water did not flow from the dream fountain because I had not yet chosen my spiritual ideals. As Elsie Sechrist suggests in *Dreams—Your Magic Mirror,* the symbol of water in this Bible passage "clearly refers to spiritual ideals, which are as necessary to the purity of the soul as water is necessary for cleanliness and survival of the body."[1]

Even though I managed to sneak past the wall into the new world without naming my ideals, I had to go back to join Mark, my life partner, and to retrieve the contents of my purse, those small but valuable blessings—such as patience, generosity, and forgiveness—which would help me to attain the ideals I would set. Mark's involvement in the naming of ideals underlines the importance of making this decision as a couple, for only through joint commitment and cooperation could we cultivate peace, love, truth, and beauty in our lives.

Twenty years ago, I had no idea what my dream self had in mind when she declared, "I want to found my own city . . . ." My head was so full of fantasy and lofty ideas, I probably thought the city symbolized some grandiose achievement: perhaps an organization that would eradicate all nuclear weapons from the face of the earth or a book that would inspire the rich and powerful to value the rights of the oppressed above their own personal aspirations. Now I know that the city of peace was the home and family that Mark and I would build together, using those simple spiritual graces I knelt to gather from where they had fallen on the ground. This may not sound like a grandiose mission, but the challenges of everyday life with a spouse and children can be so monumental that even such a microscopic "city" is unduly difficult to maintain in peace and harmony!

In building the foundation of this city, Mark and I discovered that it was essential to make sacrifices and to forgive each other again and again in order to keep peace in our home. Mark made the first sacrifice when he gave up his love of the Rocky Mountains in order to join me in Boston. Then I followed him to Birmingham, Alabama, a place I was sure I would detest, so that he could attend the surgeon's assistant program there. We thought we were making sacrifices, but each decision became an important building block in our life together. In Birmingham, our spiritual journey began in earnest; meaningful friendships were established; and a genuine love for the people, the ambience, and the culture of the South was fostered.

Just as sacrifices have to be made again and again in any relationship where two people have different ideas about what is best, forgiveness is a spiritual grace that has to be retrieved from the ground where it may be carelessly dropped many times. I have witnessed the dark side of Mark's personality, as he has mine, sides of ourselves that people outside of our family rarely see. It is not always easy to forgive the actions of this dark side, but in doing it over and over again, we express our faith in the other person. Forgiveness is our way of saying, "I know you can conquer that dark side. You *can* be the person God created you to be." Forgiveness enables us to return to the state of peace we both cherish, no matter how often it may be lost.

To pass through customs into the new world, the one where the "city of peace" would be built, I was asked to show some identification. What is my *true* identity, but that I am a child of God? "Truth" is one of the ideals that would be a necessary component of the city that Mark and I are constructing together. This city will not be complete until we learn to live *the* Truth: that God is one, and we are one with God and with all of God's children. Will we ever start to live this Truth *all* of the time, treating one another as if we were all part of the same creation?

When I run to the store to buy a tool that Mark needs for a home repair project or rake up the wood chips and sawdust that his log splitting has sprayed all over the lawn I tend, I can feel resentful about the interruption, or I can recognize that my little sacrifice is a way of giving to the whole of our relationship. All too frequently, I respond in the negative: "I'm busy!" And if I ask Mark to help serve dinner, he'll say, "I just got home from work. Can't I have a catch with Peter for five minutes?" With role models like us, we can't be surprised when the kids say, "Why me?" if we request help with a task.

But we share a lot of love in this "city" we're building, so each day we reclaim the remnants of generosity and sacrifice that may have been mislaid the day before. Mark may not help with dinner on week nights, but on

Saturday mornings, he cooks French toast or hash and eggs, and when I come home from an evening meeting, the dinner dishes have been washed. One day I'll complain about the errands and extra paperwork I have to do for Mark while he's at the health clinic, but the next day I'll take some extra time to prepare a special meal for him.

When our children, Peter and Vera, finish playing a board game together, they are meticulous in their effort to divide the clean-up chore *exactly* in half. Right now, the game of Life is lying on the floor, partially picked up, because they both thought they had already put away their fair share. Mark and I are trying to teach them that life is not about fairness, but about love, mercy, and giving. We all have trouble demonstrating this in our day-to-day lives, but we catch glimpses of that ideal life, that "city of peace," when one of us steps beyond the bound-aries of self.

Vera added a section to this ideal city when she bought a gift for Peter on a non-holiday and made a big sign for the kitchen that said: "Happy Brother's Day!" After that, Brother's Day and Sister's Day became tradi-tions in our family, always celebrated on unpredictable surprise days. Mark builds onto the city each time he sur-prises me with a home improvement project, like the time I went away for a weekend workshop and returned to find him painting the trim he had just made to put around our naked kitchen windows.

The beauty of our city-in-the-making is not so much a result of these physical improvements on our property, as it is the effect of selfless acts, performed in love. When members of a community, be it the microcosmic family or the entire family of God, allow themselves to be ruled by their hearts, each giving to the whole rather than exacting justice for every mistake, the result is a beauty too divine to capture with the physical eye. We in my family and in the society of humankind are still fledglings when it comes to this kind of life. My dream vision of the "city of peace" serves as a goal toward which I can strive until the end of my days, when the vision will be passed on to the next generation.

A couple of months before our twentieth anniversary, I dreamed that Mark and I were waiting in line to embark on a spaceship where highly evolved extraterrestrials would be teaching spiritual principles. The spaceship I fantasized about years ago represented adventure and escape from the mundane. This dream ship served a higher purpose, similar to the alien world of my "honeymoon" dream. Again we were asked to show some identification as we entered the ship, and this time there were no obstacles to keep us from "passing through customs."

Inside the spaceship, we found ourselves in a great hall, where graceful stairways with polished wood banisters led upward in different directions. I thought that it would take a very long time to explore the whole ship and find out where all the staircases went! I have had several dreams about climbing stairs in a magnificent library, transcending the lower realms of consciousness to attain the higher realms of spiritual wisdom. The numerous stairways in the spaceship must have symbolized the many possible paths to transcendence or the different roads I might follow to my spiritual destiny. I did not choose a staircase in the dream, but found myself, with Mark, in a great library. Perhaps we were able to reach this destination because the choice *had* been made, much earlier, when we set our ideals of peace, truth, love, and beauty, essential steps on the Way manifested by the Christ.

When we arrived in this library, symbol of learning and inner growth, a teacher was giving a lecture. The scene shifted to a field of sand. The teacher said that our old ways of thinking needed to change. He waved a rod over the sand, and it turned into fertile soil. Immediately a crop of lush, green plants grew in the field. The teacher said that our minds would be transformed like the sand into fertile soil, so that a beautiful new way of life could spring forth. We were also told that we who were selected for this special school would be giving birth to a new generation of spiritually advanced children. I thought, "But it's too late for Mark and me to conceive another child!" Just before I woke up, it occurred to me that Vera and Peter could be among those who would foster this new generation of "fertile-minded" children.

I felt that it was a great honor to be selected to attend classes in this spiritual spaceship school. However, we were chosen because we had made a decision to strive for those Christlike ideals, not because we had achieved them! Our teacher told us that we still had to change our old ways of thinking: all of those old ideas about limitations, competition, separateness. We know intellectually that we are one with God and all of Creation, that we are as limitless as the universe, and that what we do for one another affects every part of the cosmos. But not until we internalize these concepts and learn to live them will we transform all the barren deserts of our lives into fertile, green places.

When I awoke from that dream, I had the distinct feeling that I would return to that school for further lessons. I was filled with hope, knowing this advanced teacher (my spirit guide or, perhaps, my higher self) had faith in me and in my family. Now I have a vision of abundant, green fields to place around the city of peace as another symbol of our life's goal. And I have my dream teacher's promise that this vision would be taken up by our children and our children's children, not to be abandoned until it is made manifest in this world.

1. Sechrist, Elsie, *Dreams—Your Magic Mirror.* A.R.E. Press, Virginia Beach, Va., 1995, p. 161.

3

Finding the Balance
A Bed for Three

Stories of angelic visions, angelic intervention, and messages received from angels fascinate me. I have never seen an angel or divine messenger of any kind, but I sense them observing me from behind the invisible curtain of life's stage. When a seemingly sad scene is transformed into a happy one, I feel the energy of angelic guidance in the turn of events. I'm sure that angels or other divine messengers are responsible for some of my dreams, and occasionally I'll receive a dreamtime visit from an angelic being.

Vera was in kindergarten and Peter still at home with me when I dreamed that I was at some kind of gathering where a pretty, young blonde approached me and said that she had admired me for some time. She remembered seeing me walking with her father when I lived in Birmingham, Alabama. She had walked behind me and noticed that, when she reached out her hand, she felt a magnetic attraction between her hand and my body, a phenomenon she had not experienced with anyone else.

This dream visitor emanated a sweetness and purity such as I rarely sense in meetings with ordinary people. I believe that she was an angel, and her father, God. Perhaps it was during our stay in Birmingham that she was drawn to become my guiding angel. I think she chose to speak to me in a dream, to assure me that divine forces had been guiding me since the late 1970s, when Mark and I lived in Birmingham and we started to put some wear on our spiritual shoes.

While Mark attended the surgeon's assistant program at the University of Alabama/Birmingham (UAB) Medical School, I worked as an editorial assistant for the Southern Baptist Women's Missionary Union (WMU). I was the only non-Baptist Yankee employee, yet I was readily included in all of the potluck birthday luncheons, wedding showers, and Friday morning prayer meetings. The theology I was exposed to at work was very different from Sunday's messages at the Unitarian Church that Mark and I joined, and yet I was learning about the spiritual importance of service and social responsibility in both spheres.

On Sundays, the Unitarian minister challenged our thinking on the nuclear arms race, U.S. involvement in Central America, and environmental issues. Mark and I taught a hunger awareness class there. At WMU, I compiled "95 Shocking Facts" for *Dimension* magazine, researching statistics such as: "United States spending for defense exceeds the total income of the poorest billion people on earth." Some of the articles I edited encouraged Baptists to simplify their lifestyles, reminding them that "It is more blessed to give than to receive." (Acts 20:35) Through my work with the Southern Baptists, I became involved in Amnesty International[1] and Bread for the World.[2] I recorded in my journal: "I feel as though I am gradually crawling out of the cocoon I've been in all my life."

In Birmingham, I took up the Rosicrucian lessons I had discontinued during my graduate studies and read every Rosicrucian book in the library. It was these lessons that helped me to understand the effectiveness of prayers delivered in thankfulness and faith. In Mark's second year at UAB, he did rotations at various hospitals where he was required to work for long hours without sleep. One morning, he went to the hospital, already tired, expecting to be on his feet for as many as twenty-four hours. I decided to pray very specifically for a goal realistic enough that I could believe in it. I thanked God for arranging a two-hour nap for Mark during his rotation, from which he would awake refreshed. As I said, "Amen," I was filled with certainty that my prayer would be answered. When Mark came home the next day, he told me that he had enjoyed a two-hour nap which revived him for the remainder of his shift. Hallelujah!

By the end of our time in Birmingham, we had left the Unitarian Church where "God" and "Jesus" were deemed unspeakable words. We attended a small, informal Episcopalian church, to which we were introduced by one of my co-workers. Another friend and co-worker took us to a Unity study group, where we deepened our understanding of Jesus' metaphor: ". . . the kingdom of God is within you." (Luke 17:21)

The spiritual ideas and the citizenship lessons I gleaned from my Birmingham experience went together like red-eye gravy and ham. But none of these lessons were easy ones to remember and practice as the years heaped on us the challenges of financial stress, infertility, child rearing, and unrealized aspirations. So my dream angel came to me, thirteen years and three homes after the Birmingham "scene" of this life's drama, to encourage me to stay on the path I had been treading with *our* Father, no matter how rugged and winding that path might be.

After my encounter with the angel, the dream continued in my college dormitory room, which had just been redecorated by some friends. Debbie, one of my college roommates, was my roommate in this dream. Apparently we had been sharing two adjoining rooms, but now each of us would have a separate room. Debbie's room was a step higher than mine, decorated with a medley of hanging plants and mobiles. My room had pretty paper on the walls and a beautiful cover on a single bed. I thought, "I must try to keep this room clean; it's so pretty!" I looked at the bed a second time, and it had become a bunk bed with a double mattress on the bottom so that three people could sleep on it. I wondered with whom I would share the bed.

The day before I had this dream, I had met the mother of one of Vera's new school friends. She was an attorney, a professional woman, like Debbie, my old roommate who had become the vice-president of a big bank in New York City. Sometimes I feel inferior to women like them and wonder why I haven't achieved more "worldly success" in my life. The Women's Missionary Union was the last place I was employed on a full-time, permanent basis. Perhaps I should have gone on to become an editor or an instructor of literature at a small college. But no, God and I chose the bed that I lie in now, and it is a beautiful bed.

I was not jealous of the attorney, because I couldn't imagine being anywhere but home with three-year-old Peter, and I was involved in activities that I felt were worthwhile: coordinating volunteers and working at the community soup kitchen; participating in church committees, Bible study, and bell choir; baking cookies for Peter's nursery school. I had so many opportunities to be of service that I did frequently feel overwhelmed by all the choices. Keeping my priorities in order—God, family, others, me—was a challenge, but something I wanted to do, like keeping that pretty room clean and neat.

With two young children to care for and all of those opportunities for service, I was experiencing an imbalance in my life. There was a lot of "doing" going on and very little "being." The dream bed made for three symbolized my need to recognize all three aspects of self: body, mind, and soul. When we lived in Birmingham, I learned the importance of balancing the work of the spirit with the work of my hands. But my spirit required peace and solitude for its meditative work, and with continual interruptions from children needing a diaper change, a story, a squabble settled, or a spill mopped up, peace and solitude were available only at times when I was too tired to do anything but sleep.

I think the bed for three was a promise that the time was coming when I could again give sufficient attention to body, mind, *and* soul. I did my best to balance the various activities of life while Peter was still at home all day, even resorting to a chart where I would check off the time I spent with God, household chores, children, husband, church, social concerns, friends, and personal interests. My goal was to check something in as many categories as possible each day and to end the week with several check marks in every category. I soon discovered that life could not be balanced mathematically when some of its categories screamed louder for attention than others, and now there were so many more of them than there were when we lived in our Birmingham apartment, without the responsibilities of home ownership or children.

Just a couple of months after my dream about the angel and the bed for three, I dreamed that a friend of mine gave me a bowl of "food"—a mixture of green pepper slices, candy canes, and some yarn with which she wanted me to knit or weave the concoction together into a homogenous dish. Here was another message about my need to balance the different aspects of life. The green peppers were nourishment for my body. At first, I thought the candy canes represented a need for more play time, but candy canes are also symbols of Christ. The bent shape represents the Great Shepherd's staff, and the red stripes recall the words of the prophet Isaiah: ". . . with his stripes we are healed." (Isaiah 53:5) The white stripes symbolize the purity of the Christ Consciousness, which can be ours when we "sup with him." (Revelation 3:20)

Perhaps my guiding angel gave me this dream to remind me that I am part of the body of Christ, the yarn being the sinews that connect my body to His. When I think that I am "off balance" because I can't do many things equally well, I recall St. Paul's words in Romans 12:4-6: "For as in one body we have many members, and not all the members have the same function, so we, who are many, are one body in Christ, and individually we are members one of another. We have gifts that differ according to the grace given to us . . ."

After all, my newly decorated room with the bed for three no longer included a roommate, the one who represented the professional woman or the side of me who thought I should be out accomplishing great things "in the world." As one part of Christ's body, I could be a whole, balanced person, without performing every function needed in the larger scheme of things. In Birmingham, I had learned the importance of combining inner spiritual work with outer works of service. As a mother of young children, additional responsibilities fragmented my focus, so it was important to realize that smaller bits of service were still valuable parts of Christ's body, just as was the time spent caring for my home and family.

In my dream friend's room, the hanging plants and mobiles created a cluttered appearance. I would maintain the simple beauty of my room by narrowing the focus of my interests within the realm of prayer. The yarn in my "peppers and candy canes" dream could symbolize the prayers that linked together my various concerns. While I couldn't address the daily needs of my home and family and still have enough time for all of my personal interests and for the victims of poverty and human rights abuses, my faith in the efficacy of prayer had deepened to the point where I knew I could give many of *my* plants and mobiles to God, and they would be cared for.

Several years later, when both children were in school, another knitting dream reflected the fact that I was still struggling to balance the many aspects of my life. I was planning to sew together some knitted squares I had made for an afghan. I found that I had knitted each square using different-sized needles, so that the squares were not the same size and they did not match up. At first I thought the Dream Weaver was scolding me for not putting equal amounts of time and effort into my many endeavors. But in my morning meditation, I saw that the different-sized squares *can* fit together very nicely and make a more interesting afghan than one in which all the squares are the same. With more time to myself, the meditation and devotion squares are larger than they were when children filled the house with noise every waking moment of the day. I added a spiritual healing square when I took a Reiki I workshop. I've enlarged the "personal creativity" pieces, while the service squares are somewhat smaller in number than they once were. All of the squares are sewn together with prayer to fashion a unique and beautiful afghan that now lies on the "bed" for body, mind, and soul that God helped me to make.

1. Amnesty International is a human rights organization that focuses on securing the release of political and religious "prisoners of conscience" all over the world.
2. Bread for the World is a nationwide Christian lobbying movement that seeks justice for the world's hungry people.

4

Seed Dreams
Letting God Be the Master Gardener

$\mathcal{I}$ do not have a record of any dreams from the 1980s. This was a period of beginnings for Mark and me, a time for scattering seeds wherever we felt led. Many seeds were sown in Tennessee, where Mark took his first job as a surgeon's assistant, we bought our first house, joined numerous religious and social justice organizations, bought a piano and took lessons, gave birth to our first child, Vera, and consequently gave up piano lessons! In 1987, Mark took his second job in the emergency room of a small-town hospital in the Catskill area of New York, where we were closer to our families. We bought our second house, had our second child, Peter, and, having taken a pay-cut to move to a higher cost of living area, we cultivated prayers as a farmer would seeds.

Toward the end of 1989, we moved again, this time to the cozy red farmhouse where we still live in rural Oneonta, New York—probably the closest I'm going to get to the "cozy mountain cabin" of my college-days dream. Here we have tried to weed out those "seedlings" that don't contribute to our life's goal: to build a city of peace. I have concentrated on nurturing the seedlings of greatest value to me: Vera and Peter, my home and marriage, our church, and a few select paths of service and spiritual wisdom. One of these is the philosophy of Edgar Cayce, who recommended that we study our dreams for guidance and inspiration. So I have filled several dream journals in this decade of seed sifting and nurturing chosen seedlings. In fact, several of these recorded dreams have to do with seeds.

In September 1991, when Vera had just started kindergarten, I was reading *Discovering Your Soul's Purpose,* in which author Mark Thurston draws on the wisdom of Cayce to guide readers through a series of exercises designed to help find one's life mission. Frequently experiencing doubts about the rightness of my choices (to stay home or not, to volunteer or not, to write or not . . .), I hoped that this was *the* book that would lead me from doubt into light. One night I read examples of mission statements before going to sleep, such as "Planter of positive seeds in others' lives . . ."—my soul could relate to that one.

I dreamed that I had baked a loaf of fragrant bread, brimming with nutritious seeds and wheat berries. When I saw the bread, I realized that there might be too many seeds and not enough bread to hold it together. The next time I baked, I should not put quite so many seeds in it.

Symbolically, bread can be "food for thought," or the Christ, the bread of life. Either way, the Dream Weaver appears to say, "Spend more time in contemplation and prayer, establishing your own relationship with the 'staff of life' before trying to plant many seeds in others' lives." At that time, when Peter was still in diapers and beginning to assert *his* will in all matters great and very small, I was in dire need of a regular devotional life. If I could nurture the seeds in my own heart, I reasoned, other people would be more likely to listen to me.

I had attempted a variety of spiritual disciplines set forth by different teachers, from the Rosicrucians and Unity writers to a fundamentalist Christian who led a

Bible study near our home when Peter was a baby. I hadn't nurtured one method of prayer or meditation long enough to see what difference it would make in my attitude toward life, so a lot of little seeds were left to fend for themselves.

A year after the dream about the seed-filled bread, I dreamed that Rob, one of the copastors at the Presbyterian Church we belong to, asked me to give a report on spiritual seeds. I thought I would use the book, *The Christ Highway*, by Genevah D. Seivertson, based on the lessons given by her teacher, Eleanore Mary Thedick, a Christian mystic. These two women describe the attributes of God as seeds that lie within our hearts, which we must be willing to unfold slowly into spiritual blossoms: "All seed is alive and, according to the law of life, must come forth some time or other." The slow method of bringing these seeds to life is through trial and error, sowing and reaping. The easier way is the Christ Way . . . the Way of Grace.[1] I had gone through this book of thirty-six lessons once, but did not find the way easy, so my heart was still full of undeveloped seeds.

When it came time in the dream to give my report, I found another book in my hands: *Peace Pilgrim: Her Life and Work in Her Own Words*. Peace Pilgrim was a woman who literally walked the highway for more than 25,000 miles in order to teach others how to find inner peace as she had. Her method was really not very different from Genevah Seivertson's: to leave the self-centered life and enter the God-centered life—"the life in which you see yourself as part of the whole and work for the good of the whole."[2] In my dream, I surprised myself by speaking quite eloquently about the relinquishments made by this remarkable woman before she embarked on her pilgrimage: the relinquishment of self-will, the relinquishment of feeling separate from and judging others, the relinquishment of attachments, and the relinquishment of all negative feelings.

Next I wanted to talk about the spiritual disciplines that Peace Pilgrim undertook—her methods of prayer and meditation—but I couldn't remember them. I tried to find them in the book, but the pages had fallen out and been put back in the wrong order. The room was getting noisy. Some people were watching television. I turned down the sound, but left it on because I didn't want to be rude. I tried to continue with my talk, but people were conversing with each other. A few were still interested in what I had to say, but I couldn't make myself heard above the noise. I talked to the pastor about reorganizing the class for the following week so that only those who wanted to listen and participate could attend.

It had been several years since I'd read either of the two books featured in my dream. Before going to sleep, I had read the chapter on finding God's guidance in *Beyond Our Selves* by Presbyterian author Catherine Marshall. She writes about her attempts to quiet her mind in order to hear God's voice: "Each morning . . . I would shut the bedroom door and sit quietly, trying to still my churning thoughts. My thoughts were usually unruly: those two thank-you notes that should be written . . . Don't forget to telephone for the pick-up of the dry cleaning . . . What are we going to have for dinner tonight?"³ The disruptive people in my dream represented the inner thoughts that crowd out the "still, small voice of God" when I try to listen for His guidance. I start out with good intentions, but I frequently lose my concentration, just as I lost my place in my talk about Peace Pilgrim.

This dream also reminds me of Jesus' parable (Matt. 13:4-9, 18-23) about the sower who scattered some seeds on the path, where birds came and ate them; some on rocks, where there was not enough soil for the roots to grow in; and others among the thorns, which grew up and choked them. The seeds that fell on good soil and brought

forth grain were like the few people in my dream who
wanted to hear more about the God-centered life. Some of
these may be people with whom I can share spiritual
ideas, and some may be the seeds in my own heart that
await nurture and growth. As Genevah Seivertson and
Eleanore Thedick tell us: "Your heart's garden is . . . a
holy place, 'where the Lord can walk in the cool of the
day.' (Gen. 3:8) He gives to you His Consciousness or
direct knowledge of Him. Beloved seeker of truth, no special food, exercise, teacher, or study can ever give *this* to
you. Peace, forgiveness, faith, and love must be lived
daily."[4]

Perhaps that is why the pages fell out of my book as I
turned to Peace Pilgrim for guidance. Even Peace Pilgrim
says: "After you have read all the books and heard all the
lectures, you must still judge what is for you. Books and
people can merely inspire you. Unless they awaken something within you, nothing worthwhile has been
accomplished. But if you must read books, read many
books, so that you will contact as many conflicting opinions as possible. In this manner you'll be required to form
your own opinions after all."[5] None of the authors I enjoy
can transform *my* heart's seeds into Christ Consciousness,
just as I cannot do it for anyone else. I'm glad that Peace
Pilgrim recommends reading *many* books, since reading is
my passion. She and the authors of *The Christ Highway*
encourage me with the knowledge that my relationship
with Christ can flower even if I don't follow precisely the
methods that worked for them.

When Mark and I bought our small city farmhouse,
we inherited a little yard where Jacob's ladder, peonies,
day lilies, and other perennials bloom in turn throughout
the spring and summer. Their beauty invites me to enter
the world of nature, adding my abilities to dig, plant, fer-
tilize, and water to the mysterious creative powers of sun,
rain, and seeds. Each spring and fall, I carefully divide,

move, and arrange my plants in pleasing designs, and every year I find seedlings in garden nooks and niches where I never expected to see them. Sometimes, the wind blows seeds from neighboring gardens into mine, and the following year, I'll discover an unexpected gift among my flowers. Similarly, seeds we've sown in our lives can reappear as full-grown plants at unanticipated times.

Meeting Mark in Yellowstone when I wasn't looking for romance was an unexpected gift that changed the direction of my life. Another unexpected gift of monumental importance was the conception and birth of our daughter, Vera. Over a period of four years, Mark and I saw several doctors, read books dealing with infertility, and followed all of their instructions to achieve our goal of parenthood. I took my temperature daily, in order to chart the time of ovulation, and drugs to assure ovulation would take place each month. I underwent diagnostic surgery and then took more drugs to clear up the endometriosis the doctor had discovered. Each procedure was accompanied by prayer. At one point during this period, I conceived, only to miscarry. Following instructions had not produced a seed that would flourish.

Some months later, when the empty place in my heart was still raw with grief, a single seed embedded in this cavity whispered words of hope: "Now your longing is great enough that you can love any child God places in your arms." We had the opportunity to activate the application we had filed earlier with an adoption agency, and we were promised a baby within the year. Joyfully Mark and I set about writing our autobiographies, opening our home for inspection by the fire marshall and the social worker, and transforming our extra bedroom into a nursery. We were just as excited as we had been during the brief weeks of my miscarried pregnancy. And while we were concentrating on this new process for bringing a child into our home, Vera's life sprang forth in my womb, like an unexpected flower in a welcoming garden.

Catherine Marshall and Peace Pilgrim both suggest that we relinquish our desires in order to allow God to work in our lives. I think that Peace Pilgrim's book fell apart in my dream to intimate that I also need to relinquish some of my dependence on the particular methods of the spiritual teachers I admire. Their lessons can serve as guidance as I seek to know God's will for my life. But just as the process of growth that takes a seed from seedling to flower is a mystery, so is the flowering of our personal destiny.

A year and a half after my dream about "spiritual seeds," I dreamed that I was part of a group of people receiving sunflowers from a man who said, "One of you has been given a special sunflower that symbolizes something about that person." I looked down at my flower: It grew very bright and beautiful, then burned up as if it had been scorched by a hot sun. Nothing was left but a dried-up, brown flower, packed with seeds. It looked dead, and yet I heard a voice say, "*This* is the special flower."

The Incas worshiped the sunflower as a symbol of the sun, our life-giving energy source. The Plains Indians buried sunflower seeds with their dead to furnish food for the journey to heaven. Cardinals, white-breasted nuthatches, evening grosbeaks, and other birds have visited our feeder since we switched from mixed seed to sunflower seeds exclusively. Usually, we think of a seed as a potential source for something that will have value when it is fully manifested, but in itself the seed is worth little. The sunflower seed is a marvelous source of protein and vitamins. No wonder the Dream Weaver said that my dried-up flower was the special one!

So what did this seed-filled flower symbolize about me? At the time of this dream, I was approaching my fortieth birthday and sharing with Peter his last few pre-school months. I think the sunflower grew bright and lovely before it dried up because I was finishing a beautiful chapter of life as a mother of young children. I was on the brink of a new phase of life, full of uncertainty about the direction in which I should go. I was scattering seeds with the wind: writing articles that would be rejected, taking a temporary position on the session at church, launching a Search for God study group that would soon founder. So the gift of a "special flower" was very timely.

My previous seed dreams had shown me that I need to have faith in the mysterious process that draws a flower from a seed. As Jesus said to His disciples, "The kingdom of God is as if someone would scatter seed on the ground, and would sleep and rise night and day, and the seed would sprout and grow, he does not know how." (Mark 4:26-27) If I could remain as patiently detached from the outcome of my life's seed-sowing as I did my garden plantings, I would benefit from the sustenance of the seeds themselves, just as the birds do, while God is directing the growth of the seeds that have been buried in fertile soil.

These dreams always came during a period of uncertainty, when the activities in my life appeared more frenzied than purposeful, as I tried this and that, not knowing which thing was most likely to bear fruit. After the sunflower seed dream, when both children were in school, my contentment increased as I found time to meditate almost daily. The method I used still varied, depending on the guidance I was receiving, but the commitment to daily devotions was more important to me than the process. Vera was excelling at her piano lessons, composing little tunes of her own, so the investment in the piano and the music we created while she was in my womb proved to have a purpose. Some of my writing had been published, and opportunities to facilitate adult classes and act as a lay liturgist at church unearthed hidden talents.

Three years passed, and I went through another

period of confusion. A major crisis had ripped our church family to shreds, I was questioning the direction my private devotional life was taking, and the ratio of published to unpublished work was so small that I wondered if writing wasn't a sinful waste of time. Then I had another seed dream.

I found myself in a classroom of young children, reciting a jingle with them, the same lines over and over, so that I would remember them. When we were finished reciting, I wrote the words to the first stanza, so they were fresh in my mind when I awoke. I wrote them down immediately:

> My teacher gave me a seed—
> it was a traveling salad.
> I gave it a lot of love and sunshine,
> and a lot of rain.

I wasn't quite so sure about the second stanza, but these are the words that came to my conscious mind:

> It grew and grew and grew—
> It needed a lot of protection.
> I shaded it from the sun,
> and it grew into a tree.

My dream teacher, the Holy Spirit, or my Higher Self that's connected to the Christ Consciousness, gave me this message to assure me that each seed in my heart was growing, even during this time of confusion. The "traveling salad" image reminded me that the seed itself, like the sunflower seed, is nourishment for my soul, and it, like the kingdom of heaven, is within me everywhere I go. In spite of my confusion about events in my life and doubts about whether or not I was meditating the "right" way or doing God's will, this jingle comforted me with the knowledge that I was showering my seed with an abundance of love and care. The specifics of how I did it were of no consequence.

My dream encyclopedia says: "The seed is the sacred center out of which grows the tree of life." A tree grows much more slowly than a flower, and infinite patience is required to see the process through. I had done my best, with the resources within myself, to remain loving and just throughout the schism that cracked the framework of our church. I knew that the church's true foundation is Jesus Christ, who is indestructible, and so with love and patience, the seed He plants in our hearts will transform our church into a tree of eternal life. Likewise, the spiritual work that I do, no matter how small or uncertain each step appears to be, will eventually bear fruit. I just have to keep at it, "here a little, *and* there a little" (Isaiah 28:10), enjoying the nourishment that comes from the seed itself and not fretting about the details of the process. I leave them in the hands of the Master Gardener.

1. Seivertson, Genevah D., *The Christ Highway*. DeVorss & Company, Marina del Rey, Calif., 1981, p. 16.
2. *Peace Pilgrim: Her Life and Work in Her Own Words*, compiled by some of her friends. Ocean Tree Books, Santa Fe, N.M., 1983, p. 140.
3. Marshall, Catherine, *Beyond Our Selves*. Avon Books, New York, N.Y., 1972, p. 141.
4. Seivertson, p. 62.
5. *Peace Pilgrim*, p. 130.

5

Retrieving the Past
A Visit to Soul Space

*A*lthough I didn't pay attention to my dreams while we lived in Johnson City, Tennessee, and Walton, New York, since those years I have dreamed about returning to visit our first two homes. In one of these dreams, Mark and I went back to our Walton house, a forty-five-minute drive from Oneonta, where we observed the changes made by the new owners. These included a large garden, abundant with my favorite perennials. Then we were surprised to find how close we were to Johnson City, and we went there, too, in a matter of minutes. Time and distance pose no obstacles in dreams!

When we went to Johnson City in my dream, we didn't go to our old house, but instead visited Lee and Bill, who had been among our closest friends during that chapter of our lives. We did the same thing the two times that we really did go back to Johnson City—visit Lee and Bill, a few other old friends, and just drive by the old house to see how large the dogwoods and sugar maple we planted there had grown. After all, it's the living beings—people, gardens, and trees—to whom we remain spiritually connected after we have traded one physical environment for another.

The flora of Tennessee was what first attracted us to

that part of the country. It was April 1980 when Mark interviewed for the job he would take in the Blue Ridge Mountain area of that state. His boss-to-be picked us up at the airport and drove us past brick homes smothered by flaming azaleas. Pink and white dogwood blossoms floated like fairy lace over each lawn. I wanted trees like that in the yard of our first house, wherever it should be!

The house we bought, a two-bedroom bungalow with a coal-burning furnace, was not graced by dogwoods. However, Mark's boss's wife invited us to take some of the saplings that were crowding each other in her yard, so we dug up several and added a bit of lace to our own spring display. We also had a forsythia hedge separating our yard from the neighbors. It bloomed as early as February; then we would find the delicate blossoms encased in ice, like insects in prehistoric amber. We had daffodils in March and tulips in April, but there were several years when I had to run out and cut them all for bouquets before they were broken under the weight of a wet, spring snow.

Early springs, fried okra, hammered dulcimer music, and old friends: These are the things I miss about my Southern life. The surprise garden on my dream Walton property suggests that my nostalgia for the past may tend to glorify reality. In dreams and reminiscences I sometimes forget the long, hot summers in the South, the expansion of urban sprawl around Johnson City, and the vast distance between that place and our roots in the North. Since time and distance didn't exist in my dream, I wondered why I didn't go more often to delight in the dogwoods that bloom wild all over the Southern Appalachians in April, and talk to Lee and Bill.

When we dream, we escape the limitations of time and space and enter the Eternal Now, where all that was and will be, is. In that dimension, a visit to old friends evokes the same ambiance as did a real Saturday night get-together in the early 1980s. Mark and I would sit in front of Lee and Bill's fireplace, sipping coffee while they tucked their daughter in bed. Childless then, we didn't have to hire a baby sitter, so we could relax and stay as late as we pleased or until our hosts began to yawn. Bill was a serious mystic, not a dabbler like me. I could pick his brain for hours on subjects such as meditation, astrology, and karma. Mark and Lee joined these discussions as detached observers, then skillfully changed the subject to politics, home repairs, or jokes. Bill *said* I needed more humor in my daily life to achieve my spiritual goals, so listening to jokes was important!

Ten years after our move to New York, we drove to Florida for the kids' one-week spring break to visit Mark's father who lives there now. On the way back, we came up through Tennessee to make a brief stop in Johnson City. We drove by our old house and gazed wistfully at the dogwoods we'd planted, now full-grown. If only we could transplant them to our Oneonta yard! But we wouldn't want that steep bank in front, the one that had been agonizing to mow. Or the Bermuda grass whose endless roots had slunk silently under the borders of my first garden beds, choking the strawberry plants, sweet william, hollyhocks, and just about everything else I attempted to grow. I remember my Johnson City gynecologist joking with his nurse during one of my exams: "I finally came up with a cure for Bermuda grass: move!"

We had not moved to get away from the Bermuda grass, but to trade Mark's high-pressure orthopaedic job and the rapid demise of our rural surroundings for a small hospital in a rural village, and to be closer to our families. Still, it was painful to leave our first home and the friendships we had cultivated during that seven-year period. Lee and Bill were among those with whom our paths converged during the Southern sojourn of our life. When we moved, our paths veered in different directions. Seeing them again, ten years after our departure, we found them to be the same people we had loved, yet visiting them was not the same, could never be the same, as it used to be. They live in another house now, with new and unfamiliar furniture. We had Vera and Peter with us, and there was nothing in their house for a boy to do. We had many miles to cover before we could stop at a motel that night, so our time constraint and Peter's restlessness tugged at the edges of our thoughts as we strained to reconstruct the feeling of one of our long-ago visits.

When I saw Lee and Bill in my dream, there were no time constraints and no struggle to retrieve the same kind of friendship we used to have. We were in what John O'Donohue refers to as "soul space" in *Anam Cara: A Book of Celtic Wisdom*. There is no distance between friends in this place where souls meet, "stay attuned to each other and continue to sense the flow of each other's lives."[1]

I may not have thought about Tennessee or Lee and Bill for months before the dream that took me to see them, but like other places and people from my past that surprise me in my dreams from time to time, they are a part of who I am, whether I'm thinking of them or not. My past and future experiences are a part of my present, even though I'm not always aware of it, because all time *is* now. It follows that, if there is no time or distance in the place where souls meet, the illusion of linear time has been given to us temporarily for the purpose of our soul development. Herbert B. Puryear explains this in *The Edgar Cayce Primer*: "Since there is only One Force, since God is that Oneness, and since the Divine is Infinite, then from the point of view of cosmic consciousness, there is only one time and there is only one space. For the Infinite there is no time or space as we in our finite consciousness understand them. Yet by the grace of God we are permitted to grow in a three-dimensional awareness . . ."[2]

Beyond that three-dimensional awareness, our souls can connect with the spirits of those we can't reach in the physical world. When we sleep, we can even have some awareness of past and future relationships ordinarily beyond our ken. Sometimes I'll meet an old friend in a dream, someone I rarely think about anymore, and yet the meeting is so vivid that I sob with the joy of recognition and awaken with wet eyes. My dream visit with Lee and Bill was not quite so emotional, but I did awake with a feeling of nostalgia for that chapter of my life. During the first few years after leaving Tennessee, before my new friendships had had time to deepen, I frequently felt homesick for Johnson City. It was nice to go back in a dream and not feel like the outsider I am when we drive there with our New York license plates on our car!

In dreams and imagination, we can recapture the best parts of a past experience. Sometimes I can do it consciously. Okra in a New York supermarket is as rare as a crocus in a February snow patch. When I find some okra, I'll shovel several pounds of it into a bag, confident that the next shopper won't be disappointed by the dearth of okra "pickins." I'll take it home, slice it up to the rhythm of John McCutcheon's dulcimer hammering on his *Wry Straw* album, and shake it in a bag of cornmeal, salt, and pepper. I'll crisp it in oil while a loaf of corn bread rises in the oven. Then I'll serve it to my family, hot and crunchy, with the steaming bread and a plate of rice and beans. Fried okra, corn bread, and hammered dulcimer music make up some of the patches of the "Southern memories quilt" I wrap myself in when I want to retrieve the finest remnants of my Southern heritage.

That quilt also serves to warm me while I'm waiting for spring to come to the cold mountain city I live in now. We wait so long for the trees to bud here, I think we appreciate them all the more when they do. The tulips don't bloom until late May. If it snows then, it isn't enough to break their stems. In June, I walk to a sheltered corner where a lone dogwood blooms. Its blossoms whisper a refrain of the fairy chorus that sounds all over the white, feathered hillsides of Southern Appalachia when the wild dogwoods bloom.

1. O'Donohue, John, *Anam Cara: A Book of Celtic Wisdom.* HarperCollins Publishers, Inc., New York, N.Y., 1997, p. 10.
2. Puryear, Herbert B., *The Edgar Cayce Primer: Discovering the Path to Self-Transformation.* Bantam Books, Inc., New York, N.Y., 1982, p. 90.

6

Untying the Apron Strings
A Broom for the Journey

*A*s I think about the dreams I've had that feature my children, I recognize that much of motherhood has to do with holding on and letting go: holding on for fear of losing; letting go for fear of smothering. Mothers and children are forever seeking that perfect balance between dependence and independence.

Two days before Peter was born, I wrote in my journal that I was feeling depressed because I didn't know what I was going to do with my life besides raise children. Near the time of Vera's birth in December 1985, I had been absorbed in the details of my pending motherhood, reading baby care books, sewing accessories for the nursery, and taking Lamaze classes, yet I still found time to sand shelves for the den we had added onto our Tennessee house, answer the telephone at the crisis center, practice the piano, and go to a Peace Links benefit concert. I was too busy to dwell on how I wasn't "accomplishing" anything.

In March 1988, the month of Peter's birth, I was trying to potty train a very stubborn little girl, lugging the diaper pail down the stairs to the basement every day, and scraping food off the painted floor in the dining room of a big, shabby house in Walton, where it would be winter for another month. Since we were paying bigger bills from a smaller income than we had managed on in Tennessee, I was considering part-time job options while wondering if the new baby would nap at the same time Vera did. As it turned out, Vera gave up daily naps soon after Peter arrived, so quiet time became a rare commodity in my life. Yet, when I thought about leaving my babies with some-one else (and how pointless that would be when I would have to pay that someone to do my job so that I could go out and do another job), I knew I wasn't ready to let go, even for a few hours a day.

In February 1991, we had been living in Oneonta for a year and a half when I dreamed that a psychic predicted that The Big Flood was coming that summer, and I would be among those to drown. In the dream, I decided to med-itate to see what insight I might receive. In my meditation, I heard a radio broadcast about the flood, which faded out as a Christian song dominated the air waves. In this dream, I was working on a master's degree in literature. I thought I had completed all of the requirements, but learned that I still had to write a thesis. Now, with just a few months to live, I had to narrow my priorities. My first concern was Vera and Peter. I didn't know if Mark would survive the flood or not, so I had to plan for the children's care.

Planetary disaster usually symbolizes a threat to one's own world and signals major changes. A flood, in partic-ular, often symbolizes a spiritual cleansing or the end of an old phase in life, in preparation for a new phase. On a global scale, the Gulf War was raging at the time of this dream, and I literally feared the consequences of that crisis for the whole planet. The Christian song on the radio reassured me that God is in control, even when global disasters portend otherwise. On a personal level, I was still searching for that "something else" I was going to do with my life, and I had been talking to a career counselor at the local college. She thought there might be an opportunity for me to use my degree in women's literature to teach a course. It had been fourteen years since I received my master's, and I knew I would need to do a lot of preparation before I could even apply for a teaching position; thus, the incomplete degree in my dream.

Did the coming flood symbolize the cataclysmic change my life would undergo if I took a job? My own pending death did not frighten me, but seemed to predict a transformation from one phase of life to another. Vera was looking forward to the start of kindergarten in the fall, the first step toward "letting go" for both of us. Peter would be going to nursery school two mornings a week, and so, for the first time in six years, I would have a few quiet hours in which to rediscover, or perhaps re-create, who I was as a woman apart from children.

If the flood symbolized a spiritual cleansing rather than a cataclysm, it pointed to my ultimate decision not to pursue employment, but to delve more deeply into the creative opportunities available to the unemployed mother. Just a few days before having this dream, I had written in my journal: "I have been thinking that my marriage and children are both things that I wanted *very* much in this life. I chose them and made them a priority, so I want to keep them a priority." At the time of that writing, I thought a part-time job would enable me to keep Mark and the children foremost in my life. But I was beginning to write a little bit—a picture book and a letter to the editor about the war—and I was involved in church activities—teaching an adult class with Mark, chairing the hunger committee, playing the handbells. And I was meditating. Eventually I realized that a part-time job would consume the time I was allotting to creative and spiritual endeavors.

Later that spring, I recorded two more dreams that mirrored my seemingly conflicting need to escape some of my mothering duties while tucking my children securely into a big pocket, like a mother kangaroo would do. In the first dream, I found myself alone at a weekend retreat where I planned to do some creative work. It was just the kind of getaway I'd been longing for, but I felt lost without my children. I missed them, and my mind was void of ideas.

In the next dream, I had gone to see Mark at the hospital where he worked and left the children home alone. I thought I would only be gone for a few minutes; then, someone approached me about a part-time job opening. I started to talk to her, but suddenly I remembered Vera and Peter and ran outside. Oh! I had left my children alone in the car! The car was lying on its side. Two men had gotten Vera and Peter out. Were they trying to kidnap them? No, the men were comforting them, but I still felt overwhelmed by guilt. I hugged and kissed the kids and said, "I'm so sorry. I'll never leave you alone again." I thought the men would arrest me or at least give me a reprimand, but they said nothing.

When the children were little, I lived with an underlying terror of kidnappers that would bubble to the surface every time I saw a photograph of a missing child or when one of them disappeared from my sight in a public place. Now that they are ten and twelve, I have more confidence in their own judgment, but I remind myself that many of the murdered children I've heard about were ten or twelve when they were last seen alive. I don't think parents can ever stop fearing for their children's safety, and so those fears are the stuff of which many nightmares are made. At least this dream of mine had a happy ending, and while my children were taken from the turned-over car that might have symbolized my wounded or lopsided ego, they were safe. Perhaps the men were their guardian angels, assuring me that God cares for my children and remembers that they are my first priority, even when I am distracted by other concerns.

These dreams illumine several aspects of the "holding on and letting go" dilemma. When I visualize my children happy and secure at school or at a friend's house, I can enjoy my time alone, knowing that we will be together again at a specified time. When specters of children shot at school, snatched from their bicycles, or abused by neighbors chill my soul, I long to stuff my precious ones back in my pouch and sew it up with carpet thread.

Then there's the turned-over car. Is my ego lopsided because I allow my nurturing, intuitive side more than its share of control in my life and my children's? Or is it wounded by the gibes it receives from the various ranks of a society that no longer considers mothering and home-making to be full-time, worthwhile work? Even before Vera started school, when Peter liked to draw on the kitchen cabinets and then say, "I was just kidding," I heard the outside world clamor, "You don't know how privileged you are. You don't have to *work* like the rest of us do." Inwardly I replied, "And I don't get paid like you do, either. My children and I wear hand-me-downs; we drive a two-door, compact car, so I have to crawl into the back to get Peter out of his car seat; my sofa has holes in the upholstery." I earned the privilege of staying home by washing cloth diapers, cooking "from scratch" every night, defrosting an old refrigerator, and waxing an even older linoleum floor. Sometimes my response to a world that refers to an at-home mother as "*just* a housewife" is to hold on to my children just a bit tighter.

I don't believe that my children have been stifled by my constant presence in their lives. From the time they were babies, they looked forward to visits from baby sitters, and later, they gleefully anticipated overnight stays with friends, and going to school. Before I left Peter in his kindergarten room the first day, he went right over to the wooden boat where two boys were rocking and asked if he could join them. "Sure," they said, and stopped to let him in. Other children were crying and clinging to their mothers, but Peter and his new friends just rocked and sang, "Row, row, row your boat," as I left the room and went home to begin *my* new life as a mother beginning to let go.

When Peter was in third grade, I dreamed that he and I were on a long journey together, performing tasks and encountering many obstacles along the way. Peter was carrying a satchel that was growing too heavy. I opened it and found that it was empty. We were both relieved; now we could start collecting the things Peter really needed for this journey. The only objects I specifically remember putting in the bag were a whisk broom and dustpan. I knew that, when the satchel had been filled with all of the items Peter needed, our joint journey would be over and we would have to part. I would hug him goodbye, knowing that I would not see him again. I felt very sad, and yet I knew that parting was our goal.

On waking, I understood what the Dream Weaver was telling me: "The ultimate goal of parenthood is to 'let go' once and for all, when our children have acquired all of the values, skills, and wisdom they need to complete the journey of life on their own." Just imagining that day, when my youngest child will pack his belongings into his own car and drive away, brings tears to my eyes. Yet I know that helping him prepare for his Independence Day is part of my job.

Peter's satchel may have been heavy with unnecessary things, such as my worries about his distaste for vegetables or his stubbornness about doing a task he dislikes. When we became aware of the bag's weight, these worries must have disappeared. After all, Peter has a strength of character and a generosity of spirit that I know will increase in potency as he grows out of his childish ways.

The things he really needs are probably the same as the items that spilled out of my purse in the long-ago dream I had about going through customs to another world: patience, generosity, forgiveness, and other blessings of the spirit. So why are the broom and dustpan items of importance for this journey of life? Housecleaning is one of those occupations for which Peter has no use at all. He says, "I don't notice the dirt, and you don't have to come in my room if you don't like it." (When I heard that the other mothers were "grounding" their sons from after-school play until their homework was done, I grounded Peter until he cleaned his room. Cleanliness may not be necessary, but respecting the needs of his mother *is!*)

I learned from *A Home for the Soul* by Anthony Lawlor that since ancient times brooms have been seen as containing magical powers: "The theme of the sorcerer's apprentice who transforms a broom into a water carrier dates back to ancient Egypt . . . The Aztecs celebrated the broom with a festival to Teteo-innan, the earth goddess who swept away disease and harm."[1]

Peter may think that sweeping the floor is a bore, but he loves magic! When asked what he would wish for if he had three wishes, his first answer is always, "I'd wish to have magic powers." While Vera is absorbed in real-life dramas, Peter is reading the fantasies that once enthralled me and many more that have been written since I left that phase of life. By packing the broom in his bag, I hope I am teaching him that we can create our own magic when we sweep away negative ideas such as "I can't. That's too hard. I'm sick. I'm afraid." Remember, Peter, the witches of old, who swept away all such thoughts and flew on their brooms across the moonlit sky?

When Peter was five, he often said with a sigh, "I don't think I'll ever learn how to read." Then we'd remind him of the three-year-old Peter who had declared, "I'm going to wear diapers until I'm an o-o-old man." Now the diapers were in the rag bag, and by the time he was six,

Peter was beginning to read: the "I can" that launched him on some of the most magical adventures he would experience. Then he thought he'd never be able to ride a bike, but once that skill was mastered, too, he acknowledged that he really *could* accomplish just about anything, once he swept away his fear of failure.

Like most parents, I am learning as much from my children as they are learning from me on this journey of life. Sometimes it is Peter and Vera who show *me* how I can create magic by sweeping away the inhibitions and rigidity that years of adulthood have built up. For instance, their concept of home decor is much more flamboyant than mine. When they were little, we always had a building project as the main point of interest in our central room. It would be some combination of wooden blocks, Legos, plastic doll furniture, "Little People," and zoo animals. When we painted the children's rooms, Peter insisted on red walls, and Vera covered hers with dog posters. I stopped looking at *Country Living* magazine, with its photographs of tidy rooms sparsely decorated with antique toys. (Obviously real children don't live in those rooms.) Instead, I learned to appreciate the uniqueness of my children's contributions to my decorating scheme, such as Peter's clay cat candlestick and Vera's tissue paper butterfly.

Mark and I have taught our children to talk to God about anything that might be on their minds. We adults tend to construct taboos against certain subjects as not "appropriate" to take to God in prayer. At times, Vera and Peter have surprised and delighted us with the topics they pray about. When Peter was three, he was thanking God for every aspect of his daily life: "Thank You that Daddy and I and Vera went to the grocery store and when we came out it was raining, and thank You that I'm going to sleep with Chip [his doll] tonight." Even now, at age ten, he gives thanks for his school and each of the day's activities, including the ones he had complained about! Vera says thank you for each family member, never omitting our dog, Nero, who died three years ago. These prayers remind us to sweep away our "taboos" and give thanks for every aspect of life, including the annoying ones, like the deer who eat my plants.

This sweeping out the negative aspects of self can become a daily ritual if I examine my life on a regular basis, removing the "dirt and cobwebs" from my spiritual home. Sweeping and cleaning mean letting go of undesirable influences in order to make room for the things that are really worth holding onto. Sweeping away the clamors of the prevailing society allowed me to hold onto my conviction that staying home was the best choice for me and my family. Letting go of my fears opens the way for a deeper faith and higher hopes for my children. Cleansing ourselves of inhibitions helps my children and me to create more magic in our lives.

Perhaps if I can keep up with this daily sweeping and teach my children to do the same, we can avoid the necessity of a cataclysmic cleansing as symbolized in my dream by a great flood. And when it comes time to part ways, I'll make sure that both of my children have their whisk broom and dustpan in their satchels, because holding on and letting go are never-ending activities on the wheel of life, for parents and children alike.

1. Lawlor, Anthony, *A Home for the Soul*. Clarkson Potter/Publishers, New York, N.Y., 1997, p. 58.

7

To Find the Soul in Housework
Eating Bees and Honey

*O*h, how delightful to dwell in paradise where pure gold streets gleam, free of dust, grime, and dirt, all the way to the door of my heavenly home, where perpetual cleanliness will liberate me from the daily cycle of menial chores.

Here, in my earthly house, a kitchen wood stove requires leaving a constant sprinkling of wood chips and ashes on the floor, and children's boots leave pools of dirty water where they stack the firewood in the rack, and clothes and dishes are soiled every day, and the dog's fine, black hairs fly onto carpet, counters, and chairs. I must learn to integrate housekeeping with the spiritual, or my soul will be smothered by the monotony of meaningless activity. Can I find meaning and purpose in performing the repetitious but necessary tasks required to keep a semblance of order and cleanliness in my home?

A few years ago, I dreamed that I was in Alan Nyri's house. Alan Nyri is the man from whom we purchased our present home, so I felt that, in this particular dream, the message was about the house I live in rather than my psyche, "the dwelling place of the soul," which dream houses usually symbolize. I had taken our turntable to hook up to Alan's stereo system, but I couldn't get it to work. There was a dish containing bees and honey on the turntable, and I realized that I was supposed to eat this concoction while listening to the music. After awhile, I did hear some music, but a radio announcer was speaking, so I knew that the record player still didn't work. Now, there was nothing in the dish but a fat fly. If I could just cut off the top of the head where those enormous eyes were, I might manage to swallow the rest.

Worker bees, those busy creatures who spend their entire lives caring for the colony and collecting nectar, symbolize industriousness, organization, cleanliness— drudgery work! But the honey they produce is the sweet essence of the soul. The prophets Ezekiel and John of The Revelation are given to eat scrolls on which words of divine wisdom have been written and that taste like honey in their mouths. If only I could have nourished myself with a balanced blend of housework and soulfulness, I might have gotten the turntable to play some harmonious music that would link together my body and soul, the mundane and the spiritual. Instead, the radio announcer reminded me that I still hadn't solved my problem: how to keep up with my housework without quenching my spirit. My remaining choice was to eat the fly, that symbol of filth, without any honey to sweeten the chore. If I could remove the eyes, I might not notice just how disgusting it was.

I can always think of something I'd rather do than clean my house. The options are endless: writing projects and important books to read, church programs to prepare for, errands to run, children's birthday parties, income tax forms, friends to call. I could go on indefinitely, cutting off the eyes of that dirty fly and avoiding the issue of housecleaning, if I never make it a priority over other, more inviting or pressing activities. Even as I type these words, I've been closing my eyes to the dust and smudges on my computer. I'll clean them later. Right now it is much more absorbing to write about cleaning than to do it!

Of course, since I have acknowledged the dirt on my computer by writing about it, I have opened my eyes to its presence, and I know that I will take care of it today, or its presence will disturb my calm, like a buzzing fly. After all, the computer is an important tool that I use in my creative work. If I show my appreciation for its usefulness by cleaning and maintaining it, my soul will be satisfied that the relationship between my computer and me is balanced and harmonious.

When I was in college, I earned extra money by cleaning houses for people in the community. One of my clients was a female professor. Because it was in the seventies, when the female consciousness was being raised, this professor was probably determined not to demean herself with this lowly chore as long as there were more challenging things to do, and I'm sure her husband was, like mine, one of those eyeless flies who doesn't notice dirt. But I was embarrassed for them when I saw the black grime in their bathtub. How can they feel clean after bathing in this, I wondered, as I scrubbed and scoured to reveal the smooth white ceramic under all that "I-have-better-things-to-do" dirt.

When I cleaned houses for other people, the work was purely mechanical. In keeping up my own house, I am purifying an extension of myself and my family. The bathtub represents some of the more private functions of our bodies; cleaning it is a personal task. Bathing is also symbolic of spiritual renewal. Each time we bathe or shower, we partake in a little baptism, rejuvenating ourselves before we return to the busyness of daily life. I wish I could tell that college professor that cleaning her own bathtub would not have demeaned her, but rather would have helped her to connect with the place where she and her husband cleansed and renewed themselves, body and soul.

Okay, I stopped typing long enough to dust my PC and wipe off the smudges. This is the way I usually clean house, not making it the main job of the day, but by stealing a few moments between other activities when I can tackle one dirty little corner where the fat fly sits with bulging eyes that will *not* be removed. The big chores, such as scrubbing and waxing the kitchen floor, have to wait for the rare day when all other concerns can be set aside. This does not occur frequently enough, since the kitchen door opens into the room from a muddy driveway, another door opens from the dirt-floor basement where Mark's workshop creates clouds of sawdust, and the wood stove, cook stove, and meal debris all contrive to keep my hope of a clean kitchen out of the realm of daily possibility.

There is at least one day in the year which I am sure to set aside for the purpose of thoroughly scrubbing and waxing the blue and white square tiles in our large family kitchen. It will be a sunny day in May or June, when the ashes have been shoveled out of the wood stove for the last time, the cobwebs that stretch from stovepipe to ceiling swept down, and the stoneware and pewter pieces from the mantle washed and replaced. I'll carry the rocker and table chairs out of the room, and pile dog dishes, trash pail, and recycling box on the hearth. Before I begin to sweep, I'll put some lively Celtic music on the living room stereo, thankful for the speakers that Mark installed above the kitchen doors. The music binds my work to my spirit.

Like most housekeepers, I dread these major cleaning jobs and avoid them for as long as possible. The specter of that distasteful chore looms over me like a grimy gremlin, making it more difficult to tackle the longer I put it off. I imagine that the college professor's bathtub became just such a goblin to her, finally growing so foul that she felt compelled to hire someone to slay it, rather than struggle with the awful thing herself. As with most unpleasant tasks, I find that anticipating a major cleaning job is more upsetting than the actual ordeal. Well, sometimes I *am* angry while wrestling with that mischievous gremlin in my kitchen, knowing he'll never be gone forever, but conquering him, even for one day, can be a transformative experience.

To eat in a dream usually signifies the need for a certain kind of spiritual nourishment, or it can symbolize a transformation. When I've thoroughly swept my kitchen floor and I approach the dirt-smeared tiles with mop and pail, I can choose to feel demeaned by this lowly work or I can see it as an opportunity to partake of some bees and honey, balancing the menial side of life with the sweetness of spiritual wisdom. In some places the dirt is so imbedded in the tiles that I must get down on hands and knees to scrub the spot with a brush. In this position of humility, traditionally taken for prayer, I observe the transformation of filth into purity. Scrubbing with the music, seeing the sun's rays on the newly whitened tile, I am centered on the activity and the beauty of the moment.

This connection between body and spirit can be achieved when I have designated a particular day for the purpose of cleaning the kitchen. If my mind is buzzing with thoughts of other things I should be doing, I am more like an angry fly, beating its wings on the window. Yet, when the job is done, the floor gleaming and smelling of new wax, the gremlin has been banished, at least for the moment, and I feel a deep sense of satisfaction, whether or not I have enjoyed my blend of bees and honey.

In *A Home for the Soul,* Anthony Lawlor says:

> The most immediate way of deepening soulfulness in a home is through cleaning and repair . . . The intent of most spiritual practices, in fact, is the transformation of disorder into order.

Meditation, for example, allows the mind to transcend random excitations of thinking and gain mental coherence and peace. Yoga unwinds the tangle of stress in the body and balances the flow of energy through it . . . The word *cleaning* conveys this spiritual connotation. The roots of the word *clean* suggest the purity conferred by a ceremonial anointing with oil. Cleaning in this sense bestows a blessing on a house or apartment. It makes whole the life of the house."[1]

When I have completed a cleaning job, I sense this blessing emanating from the room where I have just expended my energy. If I managed to accomplish the task in the spirit of "bees-and-honey" connectedness, I will have enjoyed the process. Since I am a homemaker and Anthony Lawlor is an architect, I *suspect* that I am called upon to vanquish more grime gremlins than he is, and I just can't do it in meditative serenity every time. But even when I attack the dirt in my house with a vengeance, pouring my anger and frustration into a frenzy of activity, I feel blessed by the results—perhaps not in spite of, but because of, the cleansing process that constructive anger can have on my psyche. One aspect of cleaning that frequently evokes my anger is the ever-present awareness that this work is never really done, and my house will *never* be entirely clean at one time. As I'm spreading wax on my freshly mopped floor, I'll glance up at the window where sunshine reveals the drips and smears previously concealed by cloudy skies. Afterward, I'll tread the stairs, matted with dog hair, and wash my hands in the bathroom sink where soap scum rings the drain. If I'm going to balance my life with other kinds of work and recreation, I have to accept the fact that the cleaning will never all be done at once. So again, I can cut the eyes off the fly and ignore what I can't do today, or I can recognize that life is a dirty proposition and that as long as I live in this world and share my home with a long-haired dog, and people who run in and out of the door, and eat at least three times a day, the grime gremlin is going to live here, too.

One night, soon after I had completed my spring "scrub-and-wax" job, I dreamed that I was standing in line with a group of Americans who had been taken hostage by Communists. The woman ahead of me was taken into another room. When the guard returned, he gave me her shirt and told me to remove all of the buttons. Later, I would have to sew them back on! That sounded like a waste of time to me, but the guard said that they were looking for secret information under the buttons. I was relieved to see the woman come out with another shirt on, because I knew they'd be taking mine next, so the next person could remove my buttons! I wondered if and when I would be set free. A group of children were among the prisoners, and there was one whom I recognized.

What homemaker hasn't felt captive to the endless round of tasks that make up such a large part of her life? "Didn't I just do this?" we often wonder, as we scrub the same pot we scrubbed last night or pull the covers over the bed we made up yesterday. The secret information hidden under the buttons I had to remove and then replace was the clue to my deliverance: On the surface, there is no end goal to the daily rituals of cleaning the same things that we cleaned yesterday and will clean again tomorrow. But Jesus said, "In your patience possess ye your souls!" (Luke 21:19) What better way to learn patience than through the repetitious rhythm of the homemaker's life?

Not only must I learn patience with the chores I face day after day, in order to free myself from the bonds of this "labor camp," but also I must patiently accept the presence of dust and dirt as an integral part of life.

Perhaps I could do this if I become more like my children who are too busy with their creative pursuits to notice the dirt beneath their feet. The dream child I recognized among the prisoners was that part of myself that would join Vera and Peter in their little song: "Why should we clean our rooms? The dust doesn't bother us!" And then we would go out to play.

The dream child reminds me that I am captive to my housework only if I allow myself to be. The child uses her imagination to discover joy in unexpected places. Sometimes the "secret information" under the buttons reveals a capacity for joyful patience in mundane chores. When there is no joy to be found there, the child would simply put it off until later and pull out a good book or a drawing pad. The house I live in and care for can be a dwelling place for my soul, just like a dream house, if I maintain a comfortable rhythm of careful attention (bees and honey) and detachment (the eyeless fly). I may even be surprised when I pass through the pearly gates to my eternal home and find some dirty smudges on the floor. After all, if dirt is a part of life, and life is eternal, how can I expect to have one without the other?

1. Lawlor, p. 38.

8

Sharing the Spiritual Wealth
Dirty Rags in a Golden Mailbox

---

*I*n elementary school I enchanted my teachers with little stories like "Windeller, the Magic Balloon" and "Mr. Tree," about my favorite climbing tree who narrated his own life and death on the day a bulldozer came to visit our neighboring lot. Miss Scharf and Mrs. Williams told me that I had the makings of a writer, which I interpreted as "famous novelist," because, after all, that's what a real writer is! Later, when my high school counselor recommended teaching and my father suggested library science, I simply smiled knowingly to myself: I had been promised a more prestigious role on the stage of life, and I was willing to wait in the wings rather than waste my time preparing for the wrong part.

Unprepared for any particular profession, I had to sell a couple more empty paper bags to employers after Mark and I were married. During those years, I grabbed bits of time on office lunch breaks and after work to write short stories, which I mailed out to *Redbook, Mademoiselle,* and *The Atlantic Monthly.* Thousands of new writers were sending their work to the same magazines, and I soon learned the first and most important edict of freelance writing: Be prepared to cope with rejection. The only story that was accepted in those early days would

have been published in a little magazine if the company
hadn't gone out of business before my piece could see
print. Disappointing as it was, this experience showed me
that one editor liked one of my stories, and so it was not
impossible to think that someday another editor would
like something I had written.

It would be five years before my first story was published in a children's magazine. Several more successes
followed, and I thought that I had found my "niche" writing juvenile fiction. Then my children were born, and I was
astonished to find how much creative energy I poured out
for the benefit of my daughter and son. I breastfed each of
them with the milk of my soul, read to them story after
story that fed my imagination as well as theirs, and discovered the magnificence of the everyday world along with my
offspring. My journals were brimming with observations
on the unpredictability of these budding lives, my delight
and frustration with motherhood, my spiritual quest, and
my dreams, but when I put my pen to paper not bound in
a journal, my words were as dry as a teething biscuit.

In August 1992, a year before Peter entered school, I
had this dream: I told my father-in-law that I had just sold
a story for $25. It hadn't been published yet, so I decided
to show him my copy of the story. When I opened my file
drawer, I found that he had moved all of my work into
new file folders. I couldn't find the story, but he was obviously not interested anyway. He had just wanted me to
open the file drawer so that I could see what he had done.

This is the only dream I can recall having about my
father-in-law, and since he is among the least literary of
my extended family members, his appearance in this
dream about my writing is noteworthy. Vincent VanLaeys
is a businessman, grounded in the practical, material side
of life, which I've always had difficulty assimilating. At
the time I had this dream, I was planning to seek part-time
employment when Peter started school, so I thought that

the change of file folders suggested that there would be opportunities for a new and more practical vocation. Vince's lack of interest in my story indicated that I should give up my dream of being a writer.

It would be quite some time before I found a more satisfactory interpretation for that dream. First, I had to learn that I no longer had the ability to sell empty paper bags, probably because my guiding angels knew that a "regular" job would distract me from my true purpose. Then, when Peter had been in school for a few months, I realized how much I needed to be home. For the first time in eight years, I had a quiet morning hour when I could meditate and read spiritual literature. My days were full, raking leaves in the fall and shoveling snow in the winter, planning adult church classes, cleaning, shopping, recording my thoughts in my journals. And I was in the kitchen to greet Vera and Peter when they came home from school, bursting with their news about the butterflies that hatched in the classroom or the tooth that got chipped on the monkey bars.

Finally, when snow-filled streets kept me inside, reading Catherine Marshall's books and the personal essays of Linda Weltner, a stay-at-home mother and writer, I realized that, throughout the years in which I'd nurtured my children, my soul was being fed by the wellspring of motherhood. The ideas I had culled from reading, journaling, and contemplation had been taking life in the dim recesses of my being, like the wintering roots of one of my perennial plants. The time had come to shape my ideas and experiences on the page and share them with "kindred spirits." The material in my "life files" had not changed, but the way I would use it, in articles and memoirs of an ordinary life, was new to one who had always associated "writer" with "fantasy, fiction, and famous!"

By the spring of Peter's kindergarten year, I had sold two pieces and accumulated a generous serving of rejection slips, an essential ingredient in a writer's apprenticeship. I had a dream in which an unknown child was dead. The child's obituary was attached to an oval sponge which I hid in my vagina for safe-keeping. Later in the dream, some people were looking for the obituary, so I had to remove it and give it to them.

I see the child as a symbol of my creative endeavors and, in particular, my desire to write, which had been dead for so long. Putting the obituary in my vagina symbolized the potential of rebirth. The people looking for this child's death notice, which would have included its biography, were telling me that there are those who are interested in what I have to say! I took it out and gave it to them, just as I was beginning to send bits of my life story to prospective publishers.

This dream was a gift, the Dream Weaver's attempt to rescue me from the waves of guilt that periodically wash through my conscience when I think that I'm wasting time researching and writing pieces that may never be read, typing queries and cover letters, sending the same work out again and again. In the first two years that I devoted serious amounts of time and energy to writing, I sold five pieces, while fifteen others were rejected multiple times. I needed this dream to keep me afloat when those inner whisperings tormented me with reminders that a *real* job would pay me for every hour I devoted to it, that a volunteer job would be a greater service to my neighbors, and that creating special moments for family and friends would probably be appreciated more.

Most of my acquaintances don't understand the challenges of writing, the agony of searching the mailbox every day, the frustration of the rejection slips that say: "We love it, but we're overstocked," and the deflated feeling that comes with each form letter, so they tell me how privileged I am because I don't have to work in an office or a schoolroom all day. Yes, it's a blessing to be home, doing work that I love, but since I'm not devoting huge chunks of time to an employer, I find that I'm particularly vulnerable to time fragmentation. Being home means that I'm "available" for all those little events and emergencies that the employed population simply *can't* handle. If I respond to a request with something like "I'm sorry, I can't attend weekday church functions" or "I can't bake cupcakes for the school party—I have to write that day," the pause on the other end of the phone lets me know that I am self-centeredly putting my "hobby" ahead of my duties to church, family, and community.

I prefer the variety of the homemaker's life to the monotony of the office schedule I used to keep, but the struggle to gain time and recognition for my writing is ongoing. Two-and-one-half years after the dream about the rebirth of a dead child, I was still publishing a few pieces a year while dealing with a steady onslaught of rejections and wondering whether or not I should continue to subject myself to so much abuse. Then I had a dream in which I tried to push a little baby up into my uterus. It wouldn't go in, so I gave up. I noticed Peter and some other children playing on the pile of crumbly, unset asphalt where I stood. Elizabeth (a new friend) and another woman, Heather, showed up. I said "Hi" to both of them and felt pleased with myself for recognizing Heather and remembering her name.

This dream expressed the frustration I was feeling about my writing rejections and the temptation to give up and shove my creative impulses "back into the womb." The Dream Weaver was telling me that, once the flow of creativity has been released from its source, I cannot turn it off or put it back! The children, my creative energies or perhaps my unrealized potential, are playing in unset asphalt, which might symbolize unformed ideas or future projects. Elizabeth was a new acquaintance of mine who was looking to me for spiritual wisdom and guidance, such as I try to provide in my writing. Heather was a mystery, since I do not have a friend by that name. No wonder my dream self was so pleased about recognizing her! It was actually several months later when it dawned on me that Heather was the main character in a book written by Anna, a colleague in my women's writing group. Surely this dream was encouraging me to see my writing friends and spiritual companions, my real children and those born of my imagination, all cavorting together in the unformed places of my mind to provide inspiration and energy for my work.

The unset asphalt was a reminder that I was still an apprentice writer and that my growing list of published works was an accomplishment to be proud of, as was the longer list of rejected pieces, each one a stone in the foundation of my writing career. As with other kinds of life rejections—by lovers, prospective employers, people I thought were friends—writing rejections remind me that life goes on. If God closes one window, another one will open; if one idea doesn't work out, a better one will blossom. When one editor rejects a piece, the next one may love it—and *sometimes* actually find that it meets her "editorial needs"!

I treasure the spiritual message of these two dreams about children who cannot be returned to my womb. The message is one of hope, an affirmation that my creative work is valuable and important; but patience is required for the fruition of my plans and dreams, just as a mother must have patience while awaiting the birth of a baby. Since my first child came after a five-year wait that involved infertility work-ups, surgery, and miscarriage, I cannot say that I was patient, until the final six months when my burgeoning belly assured me that my hopes would be fulfilled. Waiting to see my work as a writer recognized and respected has been equally difficult. But just as I gave life to my children and continue to give them the fruits of my labors, I've learned that writing is an opportunity to give of myself to others.

My favorite chapter in Anne Lamott's book, *Bird by Bird,* is the one called "Giving," in which she says:

> You are going to have to give and give and give, or there's no reason for you to be writing. You have to give from the deepest part of yourself, and you are going to have to go on giving, and the giving is going to have to be its own reward. There is no cosmic importance to your getting something published, but there is in learning to be a giver.[1]

The reason Anne Lamott's mandate speaks to my heart, as does the dream of giving away the resurrected child symbolized by the "born-again obituary," is that she is saying, "Yes, I *can* be a writer and a giver." To give through writing is not the same as serving the hungry at a soup kitchen or talking to the desperate at a telephone crisis center, as I used to do. I did that kind of work out of a sense of duty, but I did not do it in love. When I write, I reach deep down inside myself and pull out the raw substance of my life to be crafted into a composition that will touch the souls of my readers. As I give of myself in this way, I find I have more and more opportunities to share my words, if not through publication, then by sending them to friends and fans or reading them at coffeehouses and church functions.

When I receive an acceptance letter in the mail, I leap and yell and dance around the house. The day that my first essay was published in the *Chicago Tribune,* I just sat at my desk and cried. But when I give a public reading and audience members thank me personally with an observation such as one man's—"I like the way you weave together the events of everyday life and give them meaning and purpose"—there is that quiet but satisfying warmth that comes with knowing that my soul has connected with another.

The night after the coffeehouse reading where I received this tribute, I had a dream in which I became lucid just as I was opening a golden mailbox. I reached inside and found nothing but dirty rags! For me, a golden mailbox would be full of acceptance letters from editors. To find dirty rags instead was disconcerting, to say the least! But Cinderella's rags were transformed into a beautiful gown, and my dream encyclopedia tells me that rags represent "Material poverty that hides an inner, spiritual wealth. The triumph of the spiritual over the material."[2]

I don't think it was a coincidence that the day after I had this dream, I received two acceptances—not in the mailbox, but by telephone! One was a piece I had read at the coffeehouse. I would not receive any payment for that one, but its publication in a newspaper would enable the "spiritual wealth" of that "rag" to reach more people. The other piece, "To Wait with Joy," would be published by *Horizons*, the magazine for United Presbyterian Women, and so my thoughts on living in the presence of Christ every ordinary moment of each day would be shared with 40,000 women around the country. Somehow the blessing of that knowledge *was* a greater triumph than the money I would receive for sharing the wealth of my spiritual ideas.

This triumph was probably not the kind of success my practical "father-in-law" aspect had in mind when he transferred my life's work into new file folders. Still, I am grateful to him for helping me discover the shape and voice that would propel my writing into the world. And, *if* I can be patient with the unformed creations of my imagination, portrayed in my dreams by children and unset asphalt, I may yet attain a greater balance between the spiritual and material facets of life.

1. Lamott, Anne, *Bird by Bird: Some Instructions on Writing and Life*. Bantam Doubleday Dell Publishing Group, Inc., New York, N.Y., 1995, pp. 202-203.
2. Guiley, Rosemary Ellen, *The Encyclopedia of Dreams: Symbols and Interpretations*. The Berkley Publishing Group, New York, N.Y., 1995, p. 320.

9

Judge Not the Warrior
The Silver War Medallion

When I was a child in the 1950s, my navy-captain uncle sent my family souvenirs from his world travels. Among these mementos was a brass medallion displaying the grim face of a Persian warrior, his head protected by an armored helmet, which my uncle purchased at a bazaar in Istanbul. It was not the style of jewelry my mother would wear to church or a League of Women Voters meeting, so she let me have it. I remember wearing the medallion with a skirt and sweater in high school. I guess I would have called it "funky," if funky had been a word then. Anyway, none of my friends had anything like it!

Now the tarnished medallion has hung on my wooden necklace rack, untouched for years, except by curious children's hands. I think of it as a family heirloom, but the jewelry I wear is symbolic of peace and love: hearts, angels, a silver Celtic cross, blue-and-silver earth earrings, and rose quartz stars. The grim-faced warrior symbolizes the depravity of war. So his neglected visage dangles solemnly, like a war criminal who's been judged and found guilty, condemned to hang by his neck until dead.

Dead he was, until his resurrection in a dream I had while reading *Conversations with God: An Uncommon Dialogue, Book 1,* by Neale Donald Walsch. The medallion appeared, as polished silver with silver spirals around it, then vanished. It reappeared, still shiny silver, but without the spirals. I heard the Dream Weaver's voice: "The medallion has appeared twice. Pay attention and try to decipher its message."

Because Walsch's "uncommon dialogue" was fresh in my mind, I immediately connected the dream imagery with this quote:

> The way to reduce the pain which you associate with earthly experiences and events—both yours and those of others—is to change the way you behold them.[1]

I had always "beheld" the medallion as ugly and tarnished, a reminder of war and violence, the facet of humanity that I hate and fear. In my dream, the warrior's face was as grim as ever, but how beautiful the polished silver and the graceful spirals! Spirals in a dream can represent a need for change, a growth process that is taking place, or the withering away of something no longer needed. The spirals were missing from the second vision of the medallion, perhaps to emphasize that it was time to make a change by eliminating something I no longer needed in my life. Must I let go of my judgment of the warrior and behold him in a new light—the silver light of the moon, the feminine principle, as dream silver often symbolizes?

I have hated war since I was first introduced to its horrors via the black-and-white television screen of my childhood. When I was ten, I was allowed to stay up late to watch *War and Peace*. Afterward, the images of shattered bodies clung like phantoms to my thoughts as I sobbed into my pillow, promising absolute obedience to God if only He would put an end to war forever. At eleven, I caught my first news picture of flag-draped coffins being carried off a plane from Vietnam, one after another after another. By then, I had figured out that God, who had granted free will to His foolish children, would not put an end to something we insisted was in our best interest. So I hated the warmongers, the men who held the "honor and glory" of blood and gore above the beauty and harmony of peace.

Peace became my spiritual ideal and my personal mantra. In college I learned about the Christian Crusaders and, for a time, rejected that faith which had allowed unspeakable atrocities in the name of God. Eventually I remembered the wisdom of my childhood: War is not *God's* idea, and it was not Christ's intention that people should mock His Father's name in this way. I did not have to reject *His* teachings because others had twisted and abused them. I hoped to be one of those whom Jesus referred to when He said, "Blessed are the peacemakers: for they shall be called the children of God." (Matthew 5:9)

I felt that I was beginning to earn this blessing when Mark and I joined Peace Links in the early 1980s. We participated in peace rallies, fund-raisers, debates, and forums to educate the public about the threat of nuclear holocaust. Mark and I donated what was, for us, a large amount of money to purchase a movie about the nuclear arms race so that the film could be shown at our public meetings. All I can remember about that movie now are the scenes of utter destruction, intended to convince the misinformed about the consequences of nuclear war. We thought we were doing our part as peacemakers, though later I wondered if the fear we instilled in people's minds wasn't building up the collective vision of war more than it contributed to the collapse of that evil.

In those days when our nation was supporting nuclear proliferation and war in Central America, Mark and I lived with such a sense of urgency that it seemed the only way to keep sane was to involve ourselves in every local organization that was contributing in some way to the salvation of the world. Night after night, we left our dirty dishes on the table and flew off to meet with others who shared our determination to disrupt the complacency of our friends who sat in front of television sitcoms, while rumblings of war stole around the world.

On Wednesday nights, we ate supper at the Methodist church we belonged to in Tennessee, sang hymns, and discussed the Bible, then went to the home of a Unity friend, where we joined a group of metaphysics students. This group considered topics such as "The Unity of All Life" and "Spiritual Healing." We practiced the art of positive prayer and we meditated together. Negative subjects, such as the nuclear arms race and the war in El Salvador, were never mentioned. Wednesday was the spiritual oasis in the middle of our stressful week!

At the close of the gathering with our metaphysics group, we held hands in a circle while singing "Let there be peace on earth, and let it begin with me!" I wondered how our friends could sing this song with sincerity, when none of them worked with us in the community peace movement. Didn't they see the contradiction?

In those days I judged everyone who supported the country's war machine in any way, and I judged those who, I felt, were not doing their part to dismantle that machine. I always saw myself as standing *for* peace, not as holding judgment *against* anyone. So I didn't feel the slightest twinge of remorse when I sat in church, listening to Jesus' words in Matthew 7:1-2: "Do not judge, so that you may not be judged. For with the judgment you make you will be judged, and the measure you give will be the measure you get."

Now, fifteen years later, I read in *Conversations with God*:

. . . judge not, and neither condemn, for you know not why a thing occurs, nor to what end.

And remember you this: that which you condemn will condemn you, and that which you judge, you will one day become.

Rather, seek to change those things—or support others who are changing those things—which no longer reflect your highest sense of Who You Are.

Yet, bless all—for all is the creation of God, through life living, and that is the highest creation.[2]

Reflecting back on my "social activist days," I am glad I can say that I *did* seek to change those things which did not reflect the highest sense of Who I Am or what I wanted the world to be. I have also become like some of those I once judged. This change came about gradually, after Vera was born at the end of 1985. Early on, Mark and I tried to keep up our activist lifestyle, taking our baby to meetings and setting her on the floor with some stacking cups and rattles to chew on while we discussed peace education strategies with our colleagues. But as Vera grew more active, we found ourselves taking turns going to meetings, then just staying home more and more. Sometimes when Vera was napping or quietly looking at a book, I turned inward to do my peace work in prayer and visualization of the Christ light surrounding a beautiful blue-and-white world. Then, I knew how my metaphysical friends could sing, "Let there be peace on earth," even though they never attended a peace rally or wrote a letter of protest.

As I spent more time in spiritual study and contemplation, I decided that many people praying for peace have more power to change the world than the activists with all their protests. One of my favorite quotes comes from the Virgin Mary's messages at Medjugorje: "You have forgotten, that through prayer, you can stop wars, and you can alter the laws of nature. . . ."[3]

The committees I participate in now, "Interfaith" and "Church Missions," combine spiritual and political methods of working toward peace and justice. I respect both kinds of peacemakers, their paths like two silver strands, spiraling around each other toward the goal of peace. But I've always found it difficult to respect anyone who is involved in the military.

So I was perplexed when, in 1994, an air force recruiter and his wife joined our church and quickly proved by their joyful acts of service that they were worthy of my respect and admiration. I was, at that time, our church's coordinator for the community soup kitchen, with which this couple was eager to help. One night after I had called them about serving at the soup kitchen, I had this dream: I was a nurse in training, and I had been called to spend a weekend working for one of the armed forces. A serviceman escorted me part of the way to my destination and told me that I was "under investigation." I replied, "That's okay. I'm not worried, because I have nothing to hide." He wanted me to go out with him. I told him that I had vowed *never* to date a serviceman. He left me alone, and I wandered all over a huge airport, teeming with people.

Certainly my nurse-in-training identity meant that I was learning to heal a particular conflict in my life. This seems to be a precursor to my later dream about the warrior medallion. Although I refused to "date" or befriend the serviceman in my dream, I recognized that he was a likeable person, like the air force recruiter at church. I beheld him in a new light! Was the investigation a spiritual test? I wasn't concerned about the outcome, but obviously the healing was not complete, since the man left me and I felt alone and lost in a vast place.

How can I ever really heal my feelings about war and warriors when the news from Central America, Rwanda and Somalia, Bosnia, and the Persian Gulf confirm the atrocity of war over and over? In *Conversations with God*, Walsch says, "Sometimes man must go to war to make the grandest statement about who man truly is: he who abhors war."[4]

When I remember the gentleness and generosity of the air force recruiter and his wife, long since moved to their next assignment, I know that they must abhor war as much as I do. But their response to that evil is different from mine. When my friend, Bill, read my horoscope, he said that my motto could be: "Peace at any price. My peace, your price!" Was he implying that I am not willing to make a sacrifice for peace, while those who go to war are?

Since the double dream appearance of my warrior medallion, I have sprinkled the real one with metal polish and rubbed it until it gleams again the way it must have when my uncle gave it to my mother some thirty-odd years ago. Now the brass countenance gleams brightly, but in my dream it was the silver color of the moon, the feminine aspect of the cosmos, summoning from my imagination the maiden warrior, Joan of Arc. In 1429, this young Frenchwoman wore just such a shiny helmet and coat of armor to lead her countrymen into battle against the English, who had laid her country to waste. Because she listened to the voices of St. Michael, St. Catherine, and St. Margaret, messengers of God, Joan was successful in rescuing several French cities from enemy forces, which enabled Charles VII to be crowned king of France.

St. Joan discovered that her love of God and country required her to sacrifice the peace of her home life and go into battle in order to win a far-reaching peace for her kindred. For her great courage, she earned the "rewards" of martyrdom: the torment of her accusers and the ultimate sacrifice of her life at the stake. Yes, Joan wore an armored helmet, similar to the one on the warrior medallion I had condemned to dishonor, but she bore her destiny with so much more courage than I can imagine scraping up from within my peace-loving soul.

I had forgotten the story of St. Joan while I maintained my belief that God would never support some of His children in battle against others. But I had believed Joan's story, whereas I would not have believed similar claims made by a great male warrior. I know that an eighteen-year-old girl would have no desire to go to battle *unless* she believed she had been sent by God. Her belief that God spoke to her instilled in Joan the courage she needed to surrender her personal goals for a greater cause: the liberation of her country from its oppressors.

In my sheltered life, I have never been required to call forth the full power of the lioness who sleeps in the den of my being. Still, that queen of courage has emerged, stretching and yawning, when I've needed her to help me face the challenges of my "ordinary" life: my seventh-grade classmates who taunted me for my individualism, the lesbian separatists who ostracized me when Mark came to our "cooperative" house in Boston, and some of our church friends who scoffed at our attempts to demonstrate that some of our government's acts were not supportive of peace and human rights in other countries.

I remember one church group discussion during our Peace Links days, when I declared that I would be willing to give my life in exchange for a world free from nuclear weapons. Our startled teacher responded, "Well, that's quite noble of you." At the time, I didn't think it was particularly noble: a small sacrifice for such a grand purpose. But it was an impulsive remark, made without any deliberation. I hadn't considered the manner in which I'd make that sacrifice: crucifixion, burning at the stake, hanging?

No, I had some kind of clean swap in mind: All nuclear weapons would disappear, and I'd find myself in Paradise, looking on with approval and satisfaction.

We can never know through imagination just what challenges our courage would be sufficient for. Seeing my warrior medallion in a new light, his helmet becomes the "helmet of salvation" that the Apostle Paul tells us to put on with the breastplate of faith and love (1 Thess. 5:8). Clothed in this spiritual armor, I know that God will provide me with the courage I need to face whatever situation comes, just as He gave St. Joan the courage she needed to face her enemies. Wearing this armor, I also know, through faith, that God's purpose is being worked out, even when wars and rumors of wars seem to deny that claim. His promise in Isaiah reassures me that God's ultimate plan for us does not embrace warfare:

> He shall judge between the nations, and shall arbitrate for many peoples; they shall beat their swords into plowshares, and their spears into pruning hooks; nation shall not lift up sword against nation, neither shall they learn war any more. (Isaiah 2:4)

How do I keep from judging war and warriors as evil while I await that great day? My war medallion hangs among hearts and crosses and a gold dove of peace, a reminder that sometimes the warrior acts out of love: love of family and friends, love of country, love of freedom. His is not the way that I choose to demonstrate who I am, but I can try not to judge him for choosing a different way. When he goes to war, I don't know "why this thing has to happen, nor to what end." I can occupy myself with thoughts of condemnation, or I can praise God, knowing that He will use this crisis for His purposes. At the very least, seeing the warrior in the silver light of my dream, I can realize that, without any experience or knowledge of war, we would not understand the true value and glory of peace.

1. Walsch, Neale Donald, *Conversations with God: An Uncommon Dialogue, Book 1.* G. P. Putnams's Sons, New York, N.Y., 1996, p. 37.
2. Walsch, p. 38.
3. Weible, Wayne, *Medjugorje: The Message.* Paraclete Press, Orleans, Mass., 1989, p. 209.
4. Walsch, p. 133.

10

Facing the Cross with My Eyes on the Rock

J found myself in a large public building where a wooden cross towered above a throng of people. I was to be crucified! But I knew it was just a dream. Didn't I have the power to create my own reality? I closed my eyes and imagined that I was at a warm, sunny beach. When I opened my eyes, I was still in the building and the cross still beckoned. I approached a gray-haired woman, who appeared to be the receptionist, and asked her if I could wake up so that I wouldn't have to go through with the crucifixion.

"I'm sorry," she replied, "but you must stay here and learn how to solve certain problems before you can go on to the spiritual life."

"What problems are those?" I asked. Before the receptionist could reply, Holly, Rob's wife and copastor, interrupted to tell us about some difficulties she had with her preaching. As the dream faded, I realized that I would still have to go through with the crucifixion, but I knew that resurrection would follow.

When Jesus told His disciples of His forthcoming death and resurrection, He said, "If any want to become my followers, let them deny themselves and take up their cross daily and follow me. For those who want to save their life will lose it, and those who lose their life for my sake will save it." (Luke 9:23-24) This is not an easy thing that Jesus asks of us. Whatever our daily cross may be, we can fabricate all kinds of reasons to avoid it! In my dream I thought that I could escape my dilemma by imagining myself in a more congenial environment. In waking life I can avoid the computer for days at a time, telling myself that the needs of my family, the weeds in my garden, and the bills on my desk are all more pressing than a challenging writing project. Right now I am tempted to escape to my kitchen, which *is* in need of cleaning, because this dream is so difficult to work with!

The receptionist who was my guiding spirit in this dream answered my request to wake up with a reference to "the spiritual life" for which I was not ready. I believe she was referring to "the kingdom of heaven," that enlightened state of consciousness which can be attained by *waking* from this "mean estate" where "we see in a mirror, dimly," into the *real* life where we will see God "face to face." (1 Cor. 13:12) When Jesus spoke to His disciples about taking up their crosses, He finished by saying: ". . . truly I tell you, there are some standing here who will not taste death before they see the kingdom of God." (Luke 9:27) So I don't necessarily have to wait until death to attain spiritual illumination. However, I *do* have to deal with the problems of my ego, the aspect of myself that denies my oneness with God and others, the aspect that desires a prestigious role in life, that would set me apart from the common housewife. I must give up that ego and hang it on the cross.

The receptionist didn't have a chance to explain just what problems I need to work on. Perhaps there is a clue in the interruption from the pastor who had a problem with preaching. Although I am not a preacher, I like to write and talk to others about how to live a Christlike life. I admit that I fall short of the goal myself, and so I believe I elude self-righteousness. But still, the highest form of preaching is by example, not words. In Lesson X in *A Search for God, Book I,* "The Cross and the Crown," we read that "As He took upon Himself the burden of the world, so we, in our own little world, must take upon ourselves the burdens of those about us . . . To practice, not preach, demands strength, power, and faith in the Ideal."[1]

The challenges of my "own little world" seem so petty compared to those faced by Jesus and the great saints. Some days it is a challenge to get out of bed, do my morning exercises, and assist my family in getting ready for work and school. It would be so much easier to burrow under the covers and go back to sleep! When there's a church friend to visit in the hospital or a committee meeting to attend after supper, I'd much rather stay home and keep my own affairs in order. Still, these are very small deeds, so I feel that the crosses I carry are not burdensome enough to make me a worthy disciple.

Sometimes I think the biggest obstacle to my attainment of illumination is my reluctance to accept the smallness of my world. Yet, how can I dream of bigger challenges when I grumble about the minor ones I face? When the kids are arguing over whose turn it is to brush the dog, and I'm playing referee while trying to prepare supper early so that I can get to a meeting on time, and Mark comes home late from work and chides me for letting the rice burn, my boiling blood reminds me that I am oceans away from one such as Jesus, who remained serene and humble throughout His trial, scourging, and crucifixion.

If only I could be more like Bernadette, my favorite saint, who epitomizes the humility I lack. Bernadette endured the ridicule of her family and the people of Lourdes because she obeyed the command of "The Lady," whom she alone could see and hear. Her spiritual strength, power, and faith brought forth a spring of healing waters where nothing but dry soil had existed. Those who had mocked her came to revere Bernadette as one favored by God. Yet, when she entered the convent where she would complete her short life, Bernadette told the mother superior that she could not do "much of anything," and so she was relegated to the menial work of a kitchen maid. While I complain about the mindlessness of repetitive tasks, Bernadette found joy in the act of scraping carrots. No cross was too heavy *or* too small for this truly enlightened soul.

My feeling that the services I perform are not sacrificial enough to make me a worthy disciple is often reflected in my dreams. In one of these dreams, a man holding a baby told me that he and his wife were moving to California to work at a soup kitchen because it was more challenging than the one we have here in Oneonta. By the time I had this dream, I had given up my work at Saturday's Bread, our community feeding program, because I could no longer roust enough volunteers from my church to work on the same Saturday. This dream family stung my conscience, showing me that I could find another way to participate if I chose to. The truth was that serving the "hungry" and then scraping plates half full of food into the garbage did not feel rewarding to me. Those who enjoyed the work believed that we were giving dignity to the poor by treating them as if they were in a restaurant. I decided that my family needed me on Saturdays and that I would wait until the kids were grown up before I returned to the kind of volunteer work I did before they were born. The man in my dream was holding a baby. He and his wife didn't allow parenthood to prevent them from reaching out to others.

That same night, I dreamed about the Blessed Mother Mary receiving two spiritual gifts. I couldn't remember the first when I awoke, but when it came time for her to receive the second gift, I found myself playing the part of

Mary. A cloud of light descended from above and settled onto my face. It was a divine light that would shine from Mary's face from then on. I remember thinking that she/I hadn't made any great sacrifice to deserve this gift. Of course, Mary bore a very heavy cross of her own when she accepted God's will, conceiving by the Holy Spirit at a time when an unwed mother could be stoned to death, and watching her son die a torturous death. I was the one who received the gift of light for leading an ordinary, but worthy life.

My identification with Mary the same night that I was reminded of my shortcomings as a servant of God showed me that my role as a mother is a divine calling in itself. The daily frustrations and challenges of motherhood may be very small crosses compared to those borne by Mary, Bernadette, Joan, and other saints, but they are the ones my higher self has chosen for this life, and they are big enough crosses for me. When I humbly meet the trials of my ordinary life the way Mary met her extraordinary challenges, divine light will illuminate my consciousness. It is in this daily effort to "train [my] children in the right way" (Proverbs 22:6) and to serve in the ways I feel called—whether by writing letters, leading a study group at church, or spending time with a friend—that I will gradually awaken to the *real* life. Imagining myself on a beautiful beach or fantasizing about a grander role will not provide the escape from "daily crucifixion" that I seek.

Jesus, by His resurrection, transformed the cross itself from a symbol of torture into a symbol of real eternal life. One answer to the riddle of my crucifixion dream may be that I will "escape" the burden of the cross when I learn to transform the trials of my everyday life into joyful experiences—like Bernadette did as she scraped carrots and scrubbed the floor in the convent kitchen. Sometimes I catch momentary glimpses of this kind of joy when I feel overwhelmed with love for my family and my life during the most mundane of moments, perhaps when I'm folding clean clothes for all those precious bodies.

The glimpses are harder to hold onto when I'm experiencing discomfort of some kind, such as the other day, Father's Day, when Mark's chosen activity was an eleven-mile canoe trip down the Susquehanna River. I was at the height of a summer cold, suffering malaise and congestion, and really would have preferred to stay home and take a nap. But Mark had pampered me marvelously on Mother's Day, and it was his turn to enjoy *his* kind of fun.

The first hour of the trip went well enough. It was hot, so we all slipped into the water when we reached a wide point in the river. It felt cool and relaxing to float along with the current. After we climbed back into the canoe and I had to sit in my wet bathing suit, however, I grew more and more uncomfortable. I had no idea how long it would take to reach the spot where we had left the car. Every time we rounded a bend in the river, I hoped to see a landmark. My bladder swelled up, fuller and fuller, and I was tired. The kids had been taking turns paddling in the bow. As I grew more anxious, I took over so that I could paddle a bit faster. Every few minutes, I noticed the reflection of the clouds in the serene water, a couple of geese swimming near the shore, some wildflowers blooming on the bank. Why couldn't I just appreciate the beauty of my surroundings and thank God for this experience? Because I was so uncomfortable! Because I was annoyed with Mark for leaving the car so far from our launching site! Because it was late, and I still had to prepare a Father's Day dinner. I tried to hold onto my glimpses of beauty as I shared this time with my family, but I couldn't do it. I don't have the strength of Bernadette, who never complained about her tuberculosis of the bone as she knelt on her knees to scrub the floor. All I had was a cold, and I complained.

At times like that I feel as if I have failed in my attempt to accept the smallest of crosses. But another dream assured me that Christ will lighten the burden of my cross if I share it with Him. I was visiting a Caribbean beach, sunning myself on the white sand, and swimming in the warm water. I experienced total tranquility in that place such as I have never known in waking life. When Vera was just turning one, we accompanied Mark to St. Thomas, where he attended a medical conference, but since Vera was crawling on the beach, putting sand-covered toys in her mouth, it was hardly a relaxing experience. In the dream, I was alone, without any responsibilities. A large boulder cropped out of the water. A plaque with words carved on it was attached to the rock, but it was too far for me to read it. When I saw the boulder, I thought, "I remember that. I must have been here before."

The Bible offers numerous references to God as the "rock of salvation." If I could have read the words on the plaque, they probably would have contained one of these references from Psalms: "He alone is my rock and my salvation, my fortress; I shall never be shaken" (Psalm 62:3) or "You are my Father, my God, and the rock of my salvation!" (Psalm 89:27) When Jesus told the parable of the two houses (Matt. 7:24-27), one that was built on a foundation of rock and one that was built without a foundation so it was washed away when the river flooded, the rock He spoke of was Himself. The one who built a house on that rock was one who heard Jesus' words and acted on them. The rock in my dream symbolizes the everlasting life that results from the intertwining of faith and works.

In my crucifixion dream, I could not transport myself to the beach by my own willpower. I was told that I had to work out my problems, face the cross, let go of my egotistical desires. In this dream, the beautiful beach was a gift of grace. Even though I do not always bear my cross without protest, my faith in the love and forgiveness of God is rewarded by the comforting presence of the rock. Keeping my eyes on that rock as I meet the demands that each day brings, whether big or small, I know that I am promised "the peace of God, which surpasses all understanding . . ." (Phil. 4:7)

I remembered being in that place before. I have an intimate relationship with the ocean because I grew up on the Long Island shore and visited the Fire Island beaches as many times a summer as I could pay the three-dollar fare or beg a ride over one of the bay bridges. I love the ocean in all of its moods: angry and tumultuous, happy and playful, calm and serene. Now that I live in the mountains, a trip to the ocean is a rare treat. I return with my family at least once a summer if I can. While Mark and the children ride the waves, I crash through the breakers to calm water where I lie on my back, rising and dipping with the rhythm of creation.

A dream ocean symbolizes the primordial waters, the creation of the Divine Mother. No wonder I felt that I had been there before. The union of the ocean and the rock, the Divine Father, represents that perfect state of being, the "true life" from which we all come and to which we all long to return. I know that I can go there again, because the "rock of salvation" assures me that I do not bear my cross alone.

---

1. *A Search for God, Book* 1. Edgar Cayce Foundation, Virginia Beach, Va., 1977, pp. 106-107.

11

Many Faiths, Many Paths

*W*hen I was a child, my friend, Nancy, went to Hebrew school. She showed me how to write some Hebrew words and vainly tried to teach me the correct pronunciation of "challah," the braided bread with a shiny crust and fluffy center that she shared with me on Jewish holidays. When Nancy turned thirteen, I attended her bat mitzvah at the temple.

Another friend, Louisa, took me to several events at the Church of Jesus Christ of Latter-day Saints. I learned the story of Joseph Smith and how the angel Moroni led him to the golden tablets, which he transcribed and published as the Book of Mormon. I told Louisa that I couldn't accept her church's idea that God the Father is a physical person. (By age twelve, I had given up the fantasy that I would one day sit on God's lap while He showed me illustrations of the dinosaurs the way they *really* looked.) But I respected her right to believe it if she could picture God eating spaghetti and eliminating waste like any other person.

One summer, I went to vacation Bible school with my Baptist friend, Yvonne, where I made known my belief that God the Father and Jesus, His Son, could not be one and the same Person. And I visited the Catholic Church with Patty, who lent me a little lace doily to put on my head before we entered the sanctuary. I was bewildered by the plethora of statues and candles, the aroma of incense, and the strange Latin words.

On my fourteenth Christmas, my father gave me a little book of quotes called *The Understanding Heart*. My favorite quote came from Ella Wheeler Wilcox:

So many gods, so many creeds,
So many paths that wind and wind,
While just the art of being kind
Is all the sad world needs.[1]

Having so many friends of different faith backgrounds, I found a lot of comfort in this bit of wisdom. Each of my friends was certain that her path was the straightest way to God, and since I cared for all of them, I believed that a loving God had a place in His heart for each and every one.

This childhood belief is one I have taken with me from the Congregational Church I was baptized in, to the Methodist Church I was married in, to the Unitarian Church, the first church that Mark and I joined together, to the Southern Baptist Missionary Union, where I worked in Birmingham, and to every interfaith dialogue I've had with friends and acquaintances throughout my life. The God I believe in is not exclusive.

About the same time that I joined the Oneonta Interfaith Committee, I had a dream in which I sat in the audience at a lecture hall, listening to a presentation being given by a group of people. After they had been speaking for a while, some of the presenters stated that they were Mormons and that they wished to speak to us about their faith. The audience groaned. I sympathized with the speakers and felt embarrassed for them. Why couldn't the audience listen politely to what they had to say? I did not speak, but one of the Mormons, a woman, apparently sensed my thoughts. She led me up to the platform and arranged my hair in a lovely French braid that started at the nape of my neck. She made me feel beautiful!

I have tried to make a French braid, but my hair is so fine, the result looks like a skinny sausage on the back of my head. I had no idea that a French braid can start at the nape of the neck, but some time after that dream, I found a picture of one in a hairdresser's book. To have this exquisite hairstyle created for me was such a beautiful gift, I interpreted the dream to be a message that my acceptance of different religions is one of *my* spiritual gifts.

I have never chosen to follow one particular faith or denomination to the exclusion of all others, and I don't think I ever will, because I see facets of truth in most of the religions I encounter. Each church or spiritual path meets the needs of the people who find their way to that specific strand of God's message, but we all have such diverse experiences, ideas, and attitudes about God that we have to take different approaches in seeking Him (or Her!). I have accepted Jesus Christ as my Way Shower, but I know that others have come to know God better than I have by following the path of Buddha, Krishna, or another aspect of God. This does not mean that Buddha's way is better than the way of Christ, but that others are better disciples of *their* teacher than I am of mine.

The same week as the "braid" dream, I had a whole series of interfaith dreams in one night. In the first, I was talking on the phone to a friend who belongs to a fundamentalist church. I heard her husband's voice in the background. This friend is not actually married, but I identified the speaker as Bob, a very vocal fundamentalist I had known in college. He was talking about Native American spirituality, and I was pleased to hear him say that Native Americans are children of God.

Next, I found myself in a large building where I was

going to attend a banquet. I was at the top of a staircase and noticed Nancy's mother descending. I called after her, "Can you tell me what it's like to be Jewish in New York?" She didn't answer because she was too far off by then, down in the basement. The basement reminds me that Judaism is the foundation of Christianity, the faith that I follow most closely.

In another room, I met Louisa's ex-husband, Hank, with his new wife. Before their divorce, Louisa had abandoned Mormonism for the Roman Catholic Church, and her husband had converted from the Dutch Reformed Church to Catholicism. In the dream, Hank told me that he was becoming disillusioned with the Catholic Church because he didn't understand the symbolism of the Eucharist and some of the other rites observed in that church.

Then Mark and I were cleaning up at the end of the banquet. We were servants rather than guests. A deeply religious man we know was there with his wife. This man is very concerned about Satan's activities in the world. He believes that the devil uses new age devotees, Mormons, followers of Eastern religions, and others outside the mainstream of Christianity to execute his diabolic deeds. He and his wife had fallen asleep as the banquet was ending. They had a long drive ahead of them, and I was worried that they might not be able to drive home safely.

Most of the other guests had left by then, but a man who was still there told me that he liked one of the dishes I had cooked. He told this story: He had a cup of water that refilled itself as he extended goodwill toward others. The miracle repeated itself many times. It made him feel so good that he started approaching people just to witness this phenomenon. He shook hands with three more people, and the water dried up a little bit each time until the cup was empty.

This night of multifaith dreams summons up the

imagery of Ella Wheeler Wilcox's words: "So many paths that wind and wind . . ." The man with the miracle cup discovered the essence of her message: "While just the art of being kind is all the sad world needs." When the man's genuine love for others culminated in kind deeds, his cup was full. When his motive changed from one of selfless love to a desire to see particular results, the cup dried up. Each faith and denomination offers its own ideas about the kind of salvation (or miracle) that followers can expect to receive when they express certain beliefs or live a holy life. But love is the bond that connects all faiths and all peoples, weaving us into a single, braided path to God.

There are many among my acquaintances who would tell me that I am mistaken, for after all Jesus said, "I am the way, and the truth, and the life. No one comes to the Father except through me." (John 14:6) This declaration makes for a pretty straight and narrow path for those who believe that one must call on the *person* of Jesus in order to enter the kingdom of God. But the Christ Consciousness with which Jesus *is* identified has many other names! We may call Him the "Truth," the "Way," the "Life," or the "Light." Or we may just call Him "Love." What we choose to call Him doesn't change what He is: the Alpha and the Omega, the beginning and the end; the One who invites each of us to eternal life when we follow the Way of Love. Love is the basic requirement for pilgrims who want to trod the Christ highway.

Some of my friends, like the man who fell asleep at the dream banquet, prefer to confine themselves to one narrow strip of the highway. He refuses to acknowledge those of other spiritual persuasions as children of God, so he is "asleep," incapable of grasping the full meaning of Jesus' commandment: "Do not judge, so that you may not be judged." (Matt. 7:1) He and his wife had a long road ahead of them, and if these two are dream aspects of myself, I must learn not to judge such fundamentalists or my road home will be very long, too!

Sometimes I am like Hank, the dream personage who was losing interest in Catholicism because he didn't understand it. We tend to judge people and institutions we know little about, and I grew up with scant understanding of Roman Catholic beliefs. My Protestant upbringing had taught me that Roman Catholics worshiped Mary and prayed to her and the saints, too, a blasphemous practice which broke the First Commandment. When one of my Catholic friends told me, "Mary is the mother of God," I replied, "That's impossible. God created everything and everybody, including Mary, so she can't be His mother."

I think I was eleven years old when I made that pronouncement. But it wasn't too long afterward that I learned that the pragmatic nature of Protestantism did not suit one who had always lived partially in the realm of the imagination. As a young child, I had suspected that some kind of magic existed in the real universe. As a young adult, I dipped into books such as *Song of Bernadette* by Franz Werfel and *The Blessed Virgin Mary* by Corinne Heline, and discovered that real people called mystics knew the secret of penetrating the veil between this tangible, yet temporal world and the ethereal, yet eternal. If I told my Protestant peers about Bernadette's visions of "The Lady" or the assumption of Mary into the heavenly Jerusalem, where living mystics go to join with saints and angels in the work of transferring divine energy from heaven to earth, most of them would say, "Impossible!" But having accepted the imagination as a divine gift that allows us to see beyond the limits of ordinary sight to the possibilities of life on other planes, my response to the testimonies of mystics is, "Why not?"

My discovery of mysticism led to my acceptance of Mary as queen of heaven and divine mother to all who need her. I learned in my Unity studies to pray to Father-Mother

God, because God the Creator emanates masculine *and* feminine love, an unconditional love greater than anything we can attribute to father *or* mother. When Mark and I were having trouble conceiving a child, however, I felt the need to talk to a real divine mother—one I could visualize and connect with on a personal level. So I began to pray to Mary. I learned the words to the "Hail Mary," realizing that Jesus' mother was, in a sense, "mother of God" because her Son embodied the Christ Spirit, which is one *with* God. My need for a divine mother and my belief in mystic saints made up the Roman Catholic strand I braided into my personal path to God.

Among those who recognize the divine mother's part in the scheme of Creation are the Native Americans who connect with Mother Earth as if she were a live, spiritual being. While I don't personally know any Native Americans, I have met them through books and workshops and mutual friends. I'm glad that the fundamentalist in my dream included them as children of God! Some Christians don't think Native Americans belong in God's family because of their belief in "multiple gods." But then, some monotheists think that Christians worship multiple gods in the Trinity. It all comes down to different ways of understanding the multiple aspects of a Creator too complex to be confined to a single personality or gender.

Native Americans recognize divine creativity in all of nature. They look upon plants and animals, wind and rain, as brothers and sisters to be treated with care and respect. This is different from the traditional attitude that Christians have taken toward God's instructions to Adam and Eve: ". . . fill the earth and subdue it; and have dominion over the fish of the sea and over the birds of the air and over every living thing . . ." (Gen. 1:28) We have taken the first dictionary definition for *subdue:* "To conquer and subjugate; put down; vanquish," instead of the last definition: "To bring (land) under cultivation." We have vanquished the land to such an alarming extent that soon there may be none left to cultivate, unless we learn the ways of native peoples who treat every living thing like family.

Jesus said that God is aware of every sparrow that falls (Matt. 10:29), so it feels natural to weave a love and respect for nature into the Christian faith. St. Francis sang the praises of Brother Sun and Sister Moon in his *Canticle of the Creatures* several hundred years before Europeans and Native Americans met and began to learn from one another's culture. He knew that, when Christ requested that we love our neighbors as ourselves, He was including all of Creation in the neighborhood!

I think that the banquet in my dream represented the "neighborhood" of multiple faiths coming together for fellowship. Soon after these dreams inspired me, I introduced the idea of the "Building Bridges Forums" to the Oneonta Interfaith Committee. The following year we hosted several such interfaith dialogues, where representatives of the various faith communities shared some of their practices and beliefs in order to increase understanding among them. As planning coordinator and hostess, I did not represent the Presbyterian Church to which I belong, but rather I served the whole concept of *building bridges* among people of differing views. There were some who attended only when their own church was being represented. Their absence from the other forums reminds me of the dream couple who *slept* through the end of the banquet. But there was a core group of people who sincerely enjoyed listening to the various faith lessons and gleaned some bits of truth from each of them. These were the people who realize that Jesus never said the kingdom of heaven can be found in one particular church. He did say, "The kingdom of God is within you." (Luke 17:21) Deep within the core of each soul, a place sometimes represented by a basement in dreams, no specific creeds or doctrines are necessary. Only love.

12

Jesus, How Can I Help You?

When I was eleven years old, my family stopped attending the Congregational Church where I had been baptized. We visited a variety of churches, including an ecumenical society and a Unitarian Church, where my mother hoped to be accompanied by my father, who preferred to stay home with the *New York Times* on Sunday mornings. I read *The Passover Plot* and thought I was a very sophisticated twelve-year-old when I recognized that the virgin birth, the resurrection, and all of the miracles Jesus performed could have been invented by the Gospel writers in a clever effort to procure more converts.

During my teen years, I was introduced to the ideals of transcendentalism through the writings of Ralph Waldo Emerson and Henry David Thoreau. I put away my childish idea that Jesus would give me a guided tour of heaven when I arrived there. Instead, I embraced the transcendentalists' belief that, through death or mystical ecstasy, I could achieve union with the Divine Cosmic Mystery. I would lose my Self, but in becoming one with Divine Love, Wisdom, and Beauty, I would know utter bliss.

Sometime during this period of estrangement from the Jesus I had known as a child, I dreamed that I saw Him standing on the top of a mountain, where a mighty wind whirled around Him, whipping His white robes about His body. I felt the power of that wind, and I awoke frightened. I wondered if Jesus was angry with me for abandoning Him. Then I remembered that dreams don't have any significance, and I put it out of my mind.

Eventually my study of metaphysics opened my eyes to the reality of miracles, not as supernatural wonders, but as the natural phenomena that result when we acquire a deeper understanding of God's laws. When Jesus helped Peter to walk on water, when He multiplied the five loaves and two fish into enough food for 5,000 people, when He gave the twelve authority to cast out demons and cure the sick, he was showing them that they, too, could perform miracles. Before His crucifixion, Jesus' words of comfort to His disciples included these: "Very truly, I tell you, the one who believes in me will also do the works that I do and, in fact, will do greater works than these, because I am going to the Father. I will do whatever you ask in my name, so that the Father may be glorified in the Son. If in my name you ask me for anything, I will do it." (John 14:12-14)

Many years after my frightening dream about Jesus, and fifteen years after I had accepted Jesus as my "Lord and Savior" in a Methodist church in Tennessee, I had a dream that I was applying for a driver's license in a public building where I was required to wait in several lines to see different people. The last person I saw wanted to give me a drug to show me how I would feel if I was ever "too high" to drive. He took me to another building where the drug would be administered. Once there, I realized that I was going to be used as a guinea pig in some kind of experiment. I had to get away! Aloud, I said, "In the name, through the power, and by the word of Jesus Christ, I demand that you let me go." The man released me. Several women stood between me and the door, and I repeated my prayer as I faced each one. They all let me go;

I escaped through the door and flew up into the night sky. "I did it!" I thought. Then, "No, we did it together—Jesus and I." I thanked Jesus for His help as I looked up at the stars and the crescent moon circling around in the sky. Perhaps it was a sign that Jesus had heard my prayer.

Prior to this journey to the dreamworld motor vehicle bureau, a friend had loaned me a book on angel communication. The story about the first meeting one of the authors had with his personal angel was so moving that I cried when I read it. Should I, *could* I, have such an experience myself? I had asked for a dream that would provide guidance regarding this question. Perhaps the drug test was meant to give me a spiritual "high" such as I might get from an encounter with an angel. I was warned that this kind of experience would leave me too high to drive.

As Elsie Sechrist explains, "An automobile often symbolizes the physical body, because the body is the mechanical vehicle—the 'means of transport'—of the eternal you, the soul."[1]

If I have not properly prepared my body with the disciplines of right living, a meeting with a highly spiritual being could be dangerous, like running 220 volts of electricity to a 110-volt service. This dream contained both an affirmation and a warning. I am not as spiritually advanced as one of the twelve who performed miracles in Jesus' name, but my faith in him is unwavering. If I continue to pray in His name, He will guide me through life's greatest challenges. Remembering my commitment to Jesus, who is more exalted in heaven than any of God's angels, I can look to Him as the one who shows me how to live. Then one day it will be safe for me to experience a spiritual "high" like that nocturnal flight among the stars and the crescent moon, circling endlessly about the heavens.

The thin sliver of a moon, soon to "die" and then reappear after an absence of three days, reminds me of

Christ's abiding presence throughout the waxing and waning phases of my devotion to Him. When I abandoned Him in favor of youthful skepticism, He summoned the winds of Spirit to assure me that I was His, whether I realized it or not. He knew that my heart would return to Him again and again, though I would seek spiritual wisdom from other masters, saints, and angels.

My main excuse for calling on these heavenly beings is that I long to meet a divine personage, as I know other people have, and I feel it's too presumptuous to even hope to meet Jesus Himself. While I was reading G. Scott Sparrow's book, *Witness to His Return,* in which many personal encounters with Jesus are documented, I considered praying for such an experience. Then I thought what a selfish prayer that would be, so I prayed that someone I know, whose life is empty of faith, would meet Jesus instead.

That night I dreamed that I was going about my business, whatever it was, and I saw Jesus standing silently on the horizon. It was only His silhouette, but I knew it was He, watching me, His presence assuring me that He keeps his promise: "And remember, I am with you always, to the end of the age." (Matt. 28:20) This dream taught me that Jesus not only answers prayer, but that He also answers requests that I decide I am not worthy to make! It also serves as a reminder that *all* of my thoughts are heard, including those silent judgments about people who don't live up to my standards of "right living." (Why don't they get married, if they're going to have baby? She smoked right through all three of her pregnancies. Tsk! Tsk!) I may believe that I'm righteous when I don't express my judgments aloud to others, but harnessing my thoughts is a challenge I have barely begun to meet.

In another dream, I was in a drawing class, making sketches of Jesus. We had a live model, a man who looked like the Christ. I wanted him to fold his hands, as if in prayer, but the teacher and the other students said that our pictures wouldn't look good if he did. I awoke feeling confused and disturbed by this dream. Why would my teacher tell me not to draw Jesus in prayer? I thought it might be a reminder that Jesus did not spend all of His time praying; He also used His hands to perform acts of healing, service, and compassion.

Then it dawned on me that everything Jesus did and everything that He continues to do *is* prayer. To live the kind of life that Jesus exemplified is to pray without ceasing. Even when my hands are not folded and my eyes are open, I am at prayer if my thoughts are pure and my actions are in harmony with the will of God. This may not occur very often with me, but apparently my wish to see Jesus was pure in intent since it was granted, if only in a dream.

If I learn to pray without ceasing, will I be constantly preoccupied with the needs of the world: the hungry who need to be fed, the tortured who need to be released, the lost who thirst for the waters of life? Jesus was concerned with all of these needs, but He enjoyed "little sabbaths" away from His cares, sometimes alone in the wilderness and sometimes in laughter and feasting with His friends. I witnessed the fun-loving side of Jesus through a dream that Vera shared with the family when she was nine.

Vera treasured a brown-skinned doll, which she named simply Baby Doll, "before I got good at names," she explained. Every year she celebrated Baby Doll's birthday on June 8, with little gifts she wrapped herself and a plastic cake. But it was midwinter when she dreamed that Baby Doll was a real little girl, and it was her birthday. Everyone in the family had spent a thousand dollars on gifts for Baby Doll, but when it was time to open them, we discovered that they were gone! Then, Jesus arrived at the party. Vera asked Him when *His* birthday was. He told her it was June 8 and that He was 2,050 years old.

"Why are you all so glum?" Jesus asked. We told him that Baby Doll's gifts were lost, and He exclaimed, "No wonder!"

"Can you play the piano?" Vera asked Jesus.

"Of course! I've watched Beethoven play lots of times!" He sat down at the piano and played "Happy Birthday." Then He vanished—and Baby Doll's gifts reappeared!

While Vera recounted this dream during breakfast, I kept expecting her to say that Jesus chided us for wasting so much money on gifts for Baby Doll, but He never did. From a practical standpoint, $4,000 in gifts for one person would be a scandalous waste of resources, not to mention impossible for our family. Symbolically, this extravagance represents boundless blessings poured out for Vera's most beloved possession. Why did these blessings vanish before Jesus came to the party and reappear after He left?

I can't say what it meant to Vera, but this dream event reminds me of John 10:7-10, where Jesus said, "Very truly, I tell you, I am the gate for the sheep. All who came before me are thieves and bandits; but the sheep did not listen to them. I am the gate. Whoever enters by me will be saved, and will come in and go out and find pasture. The thief comes only to steal and kill and destroy. I came that they may have life, and have it abundantly." I believe the "thief" who stole Baby Doll's gifts was the delusion that material wealth is the source of joy in our lives. Jesus, the Good Shepherd, came and cheered us with His divine presence, some light-hearted fun, and music. When He left, the gifts returned, a sign of the abundance He promises for those who choose the gate to eternal life over trust in temporal things. These gifts were not the toys and sweet treats that Vera thought she and Baby Doll would have wanted, but the gifts of the Holy Spirit that the Christ pours out for us when we demonstrate love and generosity toward one another.

When the twelve disciples gathered together on the day of Pentecost, they recognized the coming of the Holy Spirit as when "suddenly from heaven there came a sound like the rush of a violent wind . . ." (Acts 2:2) How reminiscent of the tempest I experienced in my first dream of Jesus so many years ago! Now I understand that this dream was not intended to instill fear in me, but to promise that the Holy Spirit would fill my life with blessings whenever I decided to ask for them.

"Ask, and it will be given you; search, and you will find; knock, and the door will be opened for you," Jesus promised in Luke 11:9. However, this asking and knocking on doors appears to go both ways, as He also said, "Listen! I am standing at the door, knocking; if you hear my voice and open the door, I will come in to you and eat with you, and you with me." (Rev. 3:20) Recently, I went to sleep asking for a dream with a special message that I could clearly understand. I dreamed that someone was knocking at my door. At first I thought it was a burglar, so I didn't answer. Then I realized it was probably Jesus. I wasn't certain, so I just opened the door a crack and asked, "How can I help you?" There was no reply, but I knew He was there, so I asked the same question, a little louder. Finally I spoke *out loud* in my sleep, asking "How can I help you?" and woke myself up, amazed to find myself asking this question of Jesus.

"This is not a clear message!" I complained to my Dream Weaver. "Jesus didn't answer my question!"

I have continued to be annoyed and perplexed by this unanswered question. But talk about answers to unspoken prayers! I just took a break from my writing to eat lunch and read a bit in *The New Millennium*, a journal published until recently by the Association for Research and Enlightenment. Right there, in an article written by Judith Stevens Allison, I came across these words: "All great religions emphasize that there is power in the spoken word. The [Edgar Cayce] readings suggest asking aloud three times in your morning meditation, 'Lord, what would You have me do today?'

I have prayed, "Here am I, send me, use me," almost every morning for many years, but it has been a while since I asked (and did I ever ask *out loud?*), "What would You have me do today?" I remember trying it a few times and feeling disgruntled when an idea manifested and it did not fit the plans I had already made. Now, it is *clear* that Jesus wants me to ask this or the comparable question, "Lord, how can I help You?" And I must speak out loud, just as I did in the dream when I woke myself up! Judith Allison wrote, "Those of us who have tried this exercise have gotten quite an education!" I'm sure they got a different answer to their question each day. I will try it, too, and see what surprises Jesus has in store for me.

1. Sechrist, p. 83.

13

Deliver Us from Evil
Release the Christmas Tree

As I begin this chapter, Mark is in the Dominican Republic, hammering sheet metal on roofs that were torn from hovels by Hurricane George. He and the other missionaries are clad in long pants despite ninety-plus-degree temperatures, because men don't wear shorts in the Dominican Republic. Even as plans for this trip were underway, Hurricane Mitch wrought greater havoc in Belize, Nicaragua, Honduras, and El Salvador, killing thousands of people. Hundreds of thousands of people in those countries were left homeless, but that doesn't diminish the suffering of the homeless and destitute in the Dominican Republic. Before he left with a local group of short-term missionaries, Mark said, "We'll only have time to repair a few homes, but it will make a big difference to the families we help."

The suffering that goes on every day in our world is overwhelming. Each of us deals with it in our own way: Mark by going to personally help as many people when and where he can; me by praying and writing letters from my own little corner of the world. Some years ago before I went to bed, on the eve of Epiphany, I prayed for understanding about human suffering. We were still in the midst of our Christmas celebrations, which we spread out over twelve days when the children were small and their attention span too short to keep them at the task of opening packages from grandparents, aunts and uncles, Mark and me, and Santa. I wondered how I could enjoy such an abundant life when there is now as much pain and anguish—no, more, because the human population is so much larger—as when Jesus came into the world.

As my consciousness sank into the depths of the Dream Weaver's world, I discovered that someone had removed our family Christmas tree before we were ready to take it down. Mark and I met a man who agreed to show us where some discarded Christmas trees had been taken, so that we could look for ours among them. He led us to a gloomy jailhouse where naked Christmas trees were locked up in prison cells. Strewn along the hall floor were several animal carcasses and the body of a child. None of this disturbed me because I was intent on finding our Christmas tree. We came to the end of the hall without having found it, and a door closed behind us. We were in a bare room without windows, where we thought we were going to be confined. Mark was sure the door behind us was locked, but I turned the doorknob and it opened. We headed back toward the prison entrance and passed easily through two more barriers. The man who had led us there tried to deter us, but we escaped him. We had not found our tree, but we were safe, and I felt a conviction throughout the dream that we *would* find our Christmas tree in time for the next celebration.

I think that the "someone" who took our Christmas tree and the man who locked discarded trees in prison and wanted to keep Mark and me there, too, represent the ever-present specter of suffering which tries to strip me of hope for the world. In this dream, I never lost sight of hope because I put my faith in Christ and eternal life, symbolized by the evergreen tree. It seems that the answer to my prayer was that faith and hope make it possible for one to be joyful in the face of evil, even the evil that would slay a child.

Of all the evils that afflict humanity, the abuse and murder of children is, to my mind, the most despicable. In waking life, I'm certain that I could not pass by a child's discarded body, just as I never look at a poster of a missing child or read of a child's death without offering a prayer and frequently tears. Several years ago a twelve-year-old girl from a town not too far from Oneonta was reported missing. Her face smiled at me from storefronts, car windows, and bulletin boards wherever I went. I probably prayed and wept more fervently for her and her family than I've ever prayed for anyone else. I mailed posters of her face for friends to post in other states, from Florida to Nebraska. Thousands of people were praying for her and working tirelessly to dispense the information that might lead to her safe return. I watched on television as a candlelight prayer vigil was held for this girl. Several thousand people attended.

In the end, it turned out that she had been murdered before anyone even knew she was missing. Were all those prayers offered in vain? Nothing anyone could do would have brought this child back to life, but such an outpouring of love and concern must have been a balm to her parents. I also can't help but feel that the faith and hope summoned by all those prayers contributed to the healing of this planet, just as all well-intentioned prayers do, and just as the faith and hope I had in my Christmas tree dream allowed me to focus on the gift of eternal life in the face of evil.

Faith in eternal life and the healing power of prayer help me to live with the images of abused and murdered children that regularly assault me. I can't think about some of the stories I've read without weeping, but when I'm done, I can visualize these children, joyful and whole, as they begin a new chapter in the life that never ends. I keep thinking about one particular story I read several years ago in a letter from a human rights organization. It involved the murder of a child by Salvadoran soldiers. The part of the story I want to share is what happened the night after I read it. I had prayed about this little boy— and about his brother who had witnessed his death—several times that day, not knowing how my prayers could heal a horror that had already occurred. The next morning I awoke, unable to recall my dream, yet filled with a profound sense of peace and a surety that my prayers had helped in some mysterious way to alleviate the suffering that had already been experienced.

Most of my encounters with the shadow side of life have come to me vicariously, by way of news reports or the heart-rending tales that Mark brings back from his missions trips. I have had no desire to return with him to one of these poverty-stricken areas ever since our week in a Nicaraguan refugee camp in Costa Rica, right after my miscarriage. While Mark worked in the health center, I assisted the dentist. My lack of experience was not a problem, since my job simply required that I shine a flashlight into the patients' mouths while the dentist pulled their rotting teeth and that I blot pools of blood with gauze pads. The first day, I felt faint and queasy, but I learned to perform my tasks automatically, trying not to think too much about what life would be like for those who left our care with few or no teeth. There would be no dentures for the toothless, yet we heard "Gracias" over and over because having no teeth is better than leading a life of pain.

When we left that place, where women hung their clothes to dry on barbed-wire fences and cooked their rice and plantain in old tire rims, and where people slept on cots crammed together in cinder-block buildings, waiting and wondering when the war would end, I knew that, while my presence there had made a little bit of difference in a few of many miserable lives, the vocation of mission work was not my calling. Perhaps I am deluding myself, but I believe that I can accomplish more by praying and meditating on planetary healing, by mobilizing people to walk for CROP and raise money for the hungry, and by writing letters to some of the oppressors. I find that, if I handle problems from a distance, I am less likely to fall into despair.

Mark works with suffering people every weekday, not just those with diseased bodies, but those who dwell in the dark corners of society, where rendezvous with violence, prison, promiscuity, and drug addiction are commonplace. These people look to Mark for healing and hope. They drain him of his goodwill while continuing in their self-destructive patterns. And yet, he has taken several weeks of vacation time over the last few years to travel into some of the darkest corners of the world where he ministers to people who are impoverished and desperate to extremes unfathomable by any of his patients here.

Sometimes I identify with Archie Bunker, who believed he'd get into heaven because his wife, Edith, went to church every Sunday. I can't help but think that Mark's ministry to the poor is nobler than anything I do, so I hope to get some spiritual "Brownie points" for taking care of our home and family while he's gone. I also do a lot of worrying. It's easy to imagine life as a widow when the house is void of Mark's energy day after day. I don't like it. Will I get any "credit" for this sacrifice when the tallies of "good deeds accomplished" are reckoned?

Last winter, Mark went on a mission trip to Honduras and was gone for eleven days. He called and told us that it was more than 100 degrees there. He tried to hold back some of the details that would cause me to worry, but I gathered that San Pedro Sula was a dark city, immersed in fear and hopelessness. Jags of broken bottles gleamed menacingly from the tops of the high walls that surrounded many of the homes, as well as the church where a temporary clinic was set up. A guard with an M-16 stood outside the church every day that Mark worked there. Many of the people are very suspicious of Americans. I prayed continuously for Mark's safety while he was there, but my tension was building behind a façade of faith. When he finally arrived at 3:30 in the morning, twenty-four hours later than scheduled due to airline difficulties, and crawled under the bedcovers, I clung to him while tears of relief overflowed that façade.

Later, as the Dream Weaver drew me back into her web of strange symbols and curiosities, I found that Mark and I were sharing a snack bag of mice, popping them in our mouths as if they were potato chips. I was making a little pile of the claws, but the rest was quite edible. They tasted like barbecued chicken wings. I gave one to our dog, Suzy, who was a cat in the dream, and another one to Margie, the cat who lived with us in Tennessee and disappeared years ago. When we were full, there were still two mice left in the bag, and I didn't know what to do with them.

When I thought about this scene the next day, I felt sure there had to be a connection between the mouse snack and my feelings about Mark's trip, since the dream followed his return so immediately. I wasn't surprised to learn that mice can represent the chthonic or underground powers and forces of life. The nation of Honduras represents the underworld to *me*. It was there that Mark bought the little Mayan figurine that sits cross-legged on my bookshelf. A young girl named Wendy was peddling them to the tourists. When Mark purchased two, Wendy begged him to buy more. "Maybe tomorrow," he said, thinking that he might see other interesting souvenirs at the Mayan ruins he was going to visit. "If you buy two more, my parents won't beat me when I go home," she replied. He bought two more. When I look at the figurine

I chose from the four, I imagine a waif with wispy black hair and bare feet, wandering streets patrolled by armed soldiers, wondering whether or not she'll eat supper tonight and whether or not she'll be beaten.

By eating the mice with Mark, I was attempting to digest some of the experiences he'd had in the "underworld" environment of Honduras. I think the Dream Weaver was saying to me, "You cannot be whole until you have integrated the shadow side of life with the light you want to bask in all of the time. The shadows are there, whether you choose to look into them or not. Until you face the dark, you will not totally experience the light."

Encounters with the underworld are not something I seek out, the way Mark does. But I listen to his reports and I read accounts of human rights abuses from social justice organizations. That way, I can send my prayers to specific recipients: Leticia Vargas and her daughters, brutally beaten in Tepoztlan, Mexico, because they protested the building of a golf course on sacred ground, and Wendy, a little girl selling figurines near the Mayan ruins in Honduras. These stories of hell on earth eat at my conscience; they find their way into my inner being the way mice burrow through the walls into the basement of our house. I hold them, examine them, and remove their claws so that they can't scratch my throat when I swallow them. I can digest these horror stories, these mice, if I can just prevent them from hurting me.

Mark is back from the Dominican Republic now. There is an empty canister of "chemical irritating agent," otherwise known as tear gas, on his desk to remind him of the day the missionaries had to flee the house they were repairing because a nearby demonstration broke out into a riot. The missionary workers got traces of tear gas in their eyes before they could escape the area. Because the demonstration against a company that hadn't paid its employees in six months went on for two days, Mark and the other missionaries took a day off from their construction work to distribute food to people in another village. They gave out a hundred bags of groceries, but when the food was gone, a crowd of hungry people still pressed against them. Mark is haunted by the memory of a pregnant woman holding a child, pointing to her swollen belly, and calling after them, "What about me?" as they departed for their van.

Now, the picture of this woman haunts me, too, for I've seen her through Mark's eyes. Again, I'm absorbing some of the impact of the horrors Mark experienced, so he doesn't have to assimilate it alone. Without the "claws" of firsthand experience, I can digest this kind of meat better than I might if I had been there, too. I think it's easier for me to share the burden of his pain when I'm not feeling it so acutely myself.

The mouse symbolizes a primitive aspect of the masculine principle, while cats represent the feminine principle and the chthonic aspects of the goddess. The cats eating the mice in my dream might symbolize the integration of these principles in my life: masculine and feminine, active and passive, dark and light. Mark acts on his compulsion to serve the destitute; I stay home and shovel snow from the driveway, load the wood stove, and help the children with their schoolwork. Then Mark returns and goes back to the clinic, and I pray for the hungry, homeless people in the Dominican Republic and write letters to the government leaders of Mexico, asking them to protect Senora Vargas and her daughter.

When we'd had our fill of mice munchies, there were still two left in the bag. What would we do with them? What can each of us do to diminish the evil and suffering in the world? Mark wants to improve his Spanish so that he can go back and talk to the people about the causes of their poverty. I admire his determination, but I dread the day when he will leave again for the shadowlands of

Central America. And what else can I do, here in the cozy "cabin" that I bought with my "empty paper bags"? I sought the answer in another dream:

I felt an evil presence in the house where I grew up. Three grocery bags with evil faces on them sat next to the kitchen door. The Dream Weaver told me that I could banish this evil presence and save a dying tree by saying the right prayer. I didn't know what prayer that might be, but the Lord's Prayer came to mind, so I began to recite it silently. "You have to say it out loud," the Dream Weaver instructed. I struggled to pry the sound from my throat as I said the Lord's Prayer a second time. When I reached the line "Deliver us from evil," I enunciated each word loudly and distinctly. The evil presence disappeared, and the tree survived.

The number three has many associations in mythology and religion. Since the three bags bore evil faces, I'm applying Carl Jung's theory that "three" represents the unexpressed shadow, because "three" forms a triad, and the complement of a triad is an opposite triad. Grocery bags can hold food to nurture the body, while dream bags may contain repressions. I found these bags in my childhood home, because I have been trying to repress the shadow of evil since I first learned of its existence in the words of a lullaby my mother sang to me about two children who were stolen and then lost in the woods, where they died. Robins then spread strawberry leaves over their dead bodies.

My mother says that this was a popular song on the radio when I was little. The melody was lovely, the words haunting; she sang it while rocking me in her lap. Nurtured in my mother's arms, I learned about the shadow side of life. Perhaps that's the best place to learn it, since it has to be learned some time. But I didn't know what to do about those two little children other than to cry for them.

In my dream, the Dream Weaver told me what to do for stolen children, for two dead mice, for a dying tree. I think the tree represents the World Tree, which connects the three cosmic spheres of spirit, earth, and underworld, as the tree in my yard sends its roots deep into the earth and its branches heavenward. The charge is to pray, loud and clear, to deliver all from evil! The power of prayer is mightier than any other deed that I might attempt. Just now, as I write these words, the mail brings a copy of the Lord's Prayer as interpreted by Paramahansa Yogananda, one of the preeminent spiritual figures of the twentieth century. His rendition of "Deliver us from evil" reads: "Help us to deliver ourselves from the shadowy bonds of the sole evil: ignorance of Thee." If ignorance of God is the sole evil that causes shadows and suffering among His people, then surely communion with Him is the best way to eradicate those shadows, whatever form they take. Now, when I pray for the suffering people of the world, I speak out loud, with conviction and faith: "Lord, deliver Honduras from evil. Deliver the abused and neglected children of the United States from evil. Deliver the Dominican Republic from evil! Amen."

14

To Cry Less and Laugh More

Tears spring easily to my eyes when I have a misunderstanding with a loved one or when I'm suffering a disappointment. I cry over the newspaper when I read about the death of a child, and I cry for friends who have been abused or abandoned. Sometimes tears come when I look at old photographs of my children when their cheeks were soft and round or when I sing a moving hymn with my church family. My tears soften the edges of the pain; they nourish and cleanse my soul.

A nineteenth-century hymn, written by Sarah Flower Adams, praises the spiritual necessity of tears:

> He sendeth sun, He sendeth shower,
> Alike they're needful to the flower;
> And joys and tears alike are sent
> To give the soul fit nourishment.
> As comes to me or cloud or sun,
> Father! Thy will, not mine, be done.

One morning, tears stung my eyes as I read a true story about an innocent man who was imprisoned for twelve years. He missed his daughter's wedding and saw his first born grandchild through prison bars. As the tears welled up, so did a dream fragment from the night before,

just a message that people who cry a lot exist on the surface of life. Those who are truly in touch with the Center
have little use for tears.

What a peculiar idea! I have always thought that tears
are a very natural way to express our emotions when
words don't suffice. After all, Jesus wept over Jerusalem
and He cried at the death of Lazarus. When He witnessed
the tears of Mary, Martha, and the others who mourned
Lazarus, Jesus was moved to tears and to action: the resurrection of His friend.

Likewise, our tears can move others to extend expressions of caring. When I was a freshman in college, my
roommates teased me mercilessly, shining a flashlight in
my face when I tried to sleep before they did and creating
as much racket as possible. But when a breakup with my
first boyfriend left me sobbing, one of my tormentors gave
me a warm, wet washcloth to place over my eyes. Her ges-
ture of caring touched me deeply and taught me more
about love than had my brief romance.

Sometimes, when my heart aches for the victims of a
tragedy, my prayers end in a torrent of tears. God under-
stands this wordless prayer of tears, and He soothes my
pain as I pour it out for Him. In *Pray All Ways*, a wonderful book, now out of print, Edward Hays says, "Tears are
the prayer-beads of all of us . . . because they arise from a
fullness of the heart." Public tears make us uncomfortable,
because crying expresses a lack of control. We try to sup-
press tears that threaten to disrupt our composure when
we're in a public place, and frequently we turn away when
an acquaintance gives way to tears in our company.
Edward Hays says it is that lack of control that makes
tears good prayer: "They are prayer because prayer is communion with that which is beyond our control: God." He
feels that "we should explore more ways to laugh and cry
as we worship God, or at least to allow more room for
these expressions when they arise naturally."[1]

Sometimes I am moved to tears during a worship service, and my children ask why I'm crying. Young children know tears mainly as an expression of sorrow or disappointment, so it disturbs them to see their parents cry. I can't analyze my "prayer of tears" and give them a satisfactory answer. I can only hope that I am setting a good example, so when unexplainable tears trickle down their cheeks, they will recognize the soul's need of this cleansing and not be ashamed.

Yes, I agree that tears are good prayer, so what do I do about this strange dream message: "People who cry a lot exist on the surface of life. Those who are truly in touch with the Center don't need to cry"?

Perhaps I do live too much on the surface of life, but when I cry, my tears wash that surface until it shines with such clarity, that I can see right through to the very Center of life, where the will of God is known. Seeing that Center makes it easier to find and connect with, at least for a little while.

To be in touch with the Center means to be aware of the part of myself that's connected to God: my soul. The Center is the place I seek in prayer and meditation. The Center is where I am when I make loving choices in my everyday activities. On those occasions when I can peel away the layers of emotion wrapped around that Center, I find myself in the Heart of God. Can tears exist in that holy place?

Perhaps it is in the Divine Heart that we find "the peace of God, which surpasses all understanding," of which Paul spoke to the Philippians (Phil. 4:7). A place of such indescribable peace might not include tears, for tears are the expression of nearly every emotion, but not of peace.

While reflecting on my dream, I thought of Julian of Norwich, the medieval visionary, who asked Jesus why "the great prescient wisdom of God" had not prevented sin. The Christ of her vision replied, "Sin is necessary, but all will be well, and all will be well, and every kind of thing will be well."

Julian was not satisfied with this answer, just as I was not satisfied with my dream message. She continued to question Christ and received many revelations, which she recorded in an untitled book, eventually known as *A Book of Showings to the Anchoress Julian of Norwich.* Among the "Showings" was the understanding that there is "hidden in God an exalted and wonderful mystery." At the end of time, it will make all things well. The assurance of such a supreme miracle is difficult to believe, but it is in keeping with the promises of both the Hebrew Scriptures and the New Testament:

> Then the Lord will wipe away the tears from all faces, and the disgrace of his people he will take away from all the earth, for the Lord has spoken. (Isaiah 25:8)

> . . . he will wipe every tear from their eyes. Death will be no more; mourning and crying and pain will be no more, for the first things have passed away. (Revelation 21:3-4)

"But what about tears of joy?" asked one friend, when I shared these thoughts with her. "I always cry when Lassie comes home!" Yes, most of us have felt that rush of joy and tears when something precious that was lost is found or something broken is healed. My daughter experienced this at a very young age when she discovered the long-lost head of Peter's doll hidden behind her dresser. When she ran to me, screaming, tears running down her cheeks, I was sure she'd been hurt, but she assured me, "I'm crying for joy because I found Chip's head!"

We could not feel these surges of joy if we had not first

experienced the sorrow of loss, disappointment, or despair. What will become of joy when sorrow is no more? Jesus said, "Blessed are you who weep now, for you will laugh." (Luke 6:21b) We may not cry for joy when sorrow is forgotten, but we will be happy in that time and place prophesied by Isaiah and the John of Revelation: "They will hunger no more, and thirst no more; the sun will not strike them, nor any scorching heat; for the Lamb at the center of the throne will be their shepherd, and he will guide them to springs of water of life, and God will wipe away every tear from their eyes." (Rev. 7:16-17)

Are we talking about a far-off future time, when "the Lamb at the center of the throne" will be our shepherd? The bit of dream that drifted into my consciousness, perhaps from my own ego, but perhaps from the Divine Source, gave me the sense of the Center as the Eternal Now. Contemporary mystics, such as Edgar Cayce, and some physicists, have said that all time *is* now, in keeping with scripture's imagery: ". . . with the Lord one day is like a thousand years, and a thousand years are like one day." (2 Peter 3:8)

If the "throne" is the place where we meet and commune with God, then we can find its Center, where the Christ is waiting to be our shepherd any time we are willing to lay down our burdens and take His hand. We can be in that Center *now* if we accept all of life as a gift, including the sorrows that are precursors to joy, the sins that "will be made well," and the myriad of human emotions that overlay God's holy peace. I'm sure I will continue to offer "prayers of tears" from time to time, but as I seek the Center more and more, I may find that I have little need for tears and more use for laughter.

1. Hays, Edward, *Pray All Ways,* Forest of Peace Books, Leavenworth, Kan., 1981, pp. 35-36.

15

A Marriage of Opposites
The Lake and the Sky

---

*L*aundry is one of those chores that is never done, dirty clothes landing in the basket before the last load is folded and put away, so it's no surprise that I've had a few dreams about laundry! In one of these, I was folding clean clothes on the roof of a house. A big pile of laundry fell over the edge. I pulled up some large sheets, and there was a man, my "suitor," holding onto the edge of the last one. He climbed up onto the roof and said he wanted to bake some bread for me. "The bread I will bake will be much more nutritious than what you've been eating," he told me.

At first glance, this dream appears to be a spoof on the fairy tale, "Rapunzel"! I was stuck on a roof instead of in a tower, and I pulled my "prince" up with clean sheets instead of my hair. Rapunzel was imprisoned by her witch-stepmother, who loved Rapunzel so selfishly that she didn't want the girl to meet other people—especially not a young man who might marry her and take her away. By contrast, I am already married, and sometimes feel I'm being held captive by the endless responsibilities and chores that compose a homemaker's life. Rapunzel used her hair, a part of herself, to fetch her true love, the prince who would emancipate her. I used the clean sheets from the bed I share with Mark, the foundation of our marriage, to pull up *my* savior, who offered me the Bread of Life.

Jesus taught us to pray: "Give us this day our daily bread." Our daily bread consists not only of the food we regularly require, but the obligations and challenges we must meet each day. My "daily bread" includes caring for my family—their clothes, their need to be fed, and their need for love and affection. I can look at these responsibilities as a form of imprisonment or, instead of equating the rooftop with Rapunzel's tower, I can use Edgar Cayce's symbolism of a roof as the highest point or ideals. (900-105) Remembering that my ideal was represented in a dream as a city of peace, I can use this rooftop perch to overlook the city I've been building with my family, to see how it is progressing.

Because my suitor offered to bake bread for me, I see him as a Christ figure. He said that the bread he promised would be more nutritious than what I was used to, so I interpret that to mean that I hadn't been doing my best to keep Christ at the head of my marriage and family, and consequently the city of peace was not coming along as rapidly as it might have been. I could argue with the Dream Weaver, reminding her that my family prays regularly together at meals and bedtime, we attend church together, and we frequently discuss matters of spiritual import. Then the Dream Weaver would retort, "But look at all the disharmony in this family! I can understand the kids arguing about whose turn it is to brush the dog, but what about you and Mark? You're so resentful when he wants to go off on a mission trip, or skiing, or hang gliding, but you don't want to do any of those things yourself. And then he ridicules so many of your spiritual ideas, but he's too busy to read the books that have helped you to formulate these views."

Well, yes, I have to admit that while we share the same

ideals, Mark and I have very different approaches to life, which can create friction in our relationship from time to time. Mark is a "doer," the kind of person who isn't content unless he's active, running, hiking, building a fence, splitting firewood. He does everything at top speed. When we go for a walk together, I have to trot to keep up with him. He does manage to sit still for his morning devotions, but I know his mind is racing as he tries to include all of his concerns for family, friends, patients, and world problems in every prayer. The only time he can "Be still and know that I am God" (Psalm 46:11) is when he's winging above the treetops, the wind hushing every other sound from the sky.

Mark's nickname for me is "Bean," a seemingly meaningless endearment, except that it almost sounds like "being." While Mark is the doer in our relationship, I am the one who just likes to "be"—be alone with a cup of tea, be reading in the kitchen rocker, be digging in my garden. These are all activities, but most of the things I do are contemplative. Recently I took up lap swimming at the YMCA, a contemplative form of exercise. Rhythmically pushing my body through the yielding water is a tranquil way to strengthen my heart. And I don't sweat!

It is commonly believed that "opposites attract," and there is a good reason for this. In a union of opposites, two partners learn to balance one another's strengths and shortcomings. With much effort on both parts, we can learn from each other and grow as individuals as we strengthen our marriage. Sometimes my dreams offer guidance for this perpetual struggle of my yin and Mark's yang to maintain harmony so that our city of peace can thrive.

In one such dream, Mark and I were guests at an elegant inn, where we were receiving free room and board in exchange for Mark's work with a man who was deaf and mute. Mark was teaching the man to speak and helping him in other ways. Because of Mark's work as a physician's assistant, I have accompanied him to several medical conferences held at resorts or inns far more luxurious than we could ever manage on our own finances. On a spiritual level, an inn reminds us of the parable in Luke 10:25-32, in which a man who had been beaten and robbed was taken to an inn by the Samaritan, who paid for his care. I'm afraid I am like the priest in that story, all wrapped up in my spiritual reading, prayer, and contemplation, passing by the suffering soul who might live right in my neighborhood. Mark is the one who serves those in need, because he is a *doer*, and we both benefit from the work he does. He must heal the man who is *deaf*, one who is unreceptive to the divine voice within, because Mark needs to hear its message, just as I need to act on the messages I hear.

There was a swimming pool at the inn, but I decided to swim in a nearby lake. I found myself in the lake with Mark and a lot of other people, at least some of whom were members of our church. A large, oceanlike wave swelled under the group, lifting us up and bringing us back down. Then I saw a tsunami heading toward me! I was frightened, but I rode it easily, this time alone, as it crested in the sky, which had turned from day to night. What fun! But I was afraid of crashing down. I landed safely, way out in the middle of the lake, far from the crowd. The current took me even farther away, but I swam out of it and back to the others. The first person I came to was Mark. I put my arms around him, feeling safe, and woke up. When I drifted back to sleep, I returned to the inn, where I saw Evie, a church friend. She asked me why I hadn't called her in a few days and I said, "I've been swimming."

According to Edgar Cayce, swimming symbolizes spiritual activity, while intuition author Rosemary Ellen

Guiley says that a dream swimmer is "navigating through the waters of the unconscious."[1] Guiley's interpretation also implies that, by swimming in a vast lake, I was opening up more uncharted territories in my unconscious than I would if I had chosen to swim in the manmade pool. At the time this dream came to me, I was, in fact, delving deep into my unconscious: meditating, recording and working with my dreams, and communicating with spiritual counselors who believed they put me in touch with my inner Self—and maybe they did. My spiritual reading and prayer life, to which I had added the use of rosary beads and incense, took me a tidal wave away from what was acceptable to Mark and most of our church's congregation.

In our relationship, Mark is the one who seeks out adventure, frequently involving physical risk. Last winter, he and a friend camped on the top of a mountain in the snow. Neither of them slept at all, they were so cold. This year he's been taking hang gliding lessons, taking every precaution to fly safely, but it's still an unnecessary risk in *my* opinion. For him it *is* necessary, for part of his soul has been in the clouds since his youth, when he used his newspaper route earnings to pay for flying lessons and rode his bike ten miles to the airport once a month for that purpose.

When it comes to religion, Mark is the cautious one, his faith in a loving God partially eclipsed by that aura of infallibility that surrounds the Bible and its interpretation by the vocal majority of Christians. When we attended a spirituality retreat sponsored by the Presbyterian Church, I was thrilled to hear a leader in my own denomination give approval to those of us who want to address God as Spirit, Mother, Divine Mystery—or any name that helps us to better understand the Supreme Being. Mark still doesn't think we should call God by any name that isn't used in the Bible, but his narrow view can't prevent my seeking new ways to imagine and identify God in my private meditations, symbolized by that lone swim on the crest of a tsunami that took me up to the stars.

Mark eagerly returns to me and the children after one of his forays to the top of a mountain, the depths of Central American poverty, or the clouds. We wait here for him and listen to every detail of his escapades, sometimes sharing his excitement, other times horrified by a close call. The hang glider with all of its supplemental paraphernalia has spawned the first serious financial disagreement in our marriage, and sometimes dampens my ability to generate enthusiasm for his adventures.

Likewise, I return from my spiritual explorations to "prayers as usual" with Mark and the children, who prefer to "swim" with our church family in tamer waters. I bring with me bits and pieces of concepts from my reading and contemplation. Some are considered, others are met with skepticism. They don't like the written prayers and affirmations I use, even though we recited "Now I lay me down to sleep . . ." for years. The children agree that a loving God wouldn't send people to an eternity in hell because they don't believe that Jesus died for their sins. Mark concedes that this doesn't make sense, but he thinks we have to be careful about rejecting parts of the Bible just because we don't like them. I tell him I'm just rejecting the parts that don't conform to the *spirit* of God's law, which is love, but he refers to this as "cafeteria-style" religion.

While I complain about the physical and financial risks Mark takes, his main complaint about my spiritual explorations is that I believe everything I read indiscriminately. I have pointed out to him that this is not possible, given that I read many ideas that contradict each other, just as sections of the Bible are conflictive if taken literally. Among the concepts I believe in, to Mark's chagrin, are chakras (the spiritual centers of the body), nature spirits, and auras. The existence of these and other phenomena that can't be seen by the average person are widely accepted in metaphysical circles and plainly visible to clairvoyants. I have a friend who perceives auras, and when we meditate together, she sees my body grow transparent and my face dissolve into a pool of light. My vision is restricted to the same three-dimensional world that Mark's is. I've never beheld a deva, an angel, or any astral entity, but I can easily accept their existence because countless others *have* seen them, and I know God's great universe must contain all kinds of wonders we earthlings can't begin to imagine.

Mark prevents me from dwelling too much on the crests of tidal waves, speculating on these marvels that fill me with awe, but that don't help me deal with the nitty-gritties of life. He is the one who taught me to drive a stick-shift, change a tire, paddle a canoe, and handle tools, among other skills that help me to function on the physical plane that I share with him. When we hike through a forest together, I make him slow down and observe the wildflowers and mushrooms he passes over in his hurry to reach the top of the mountain or the end of the trail. So I learn from his yang as he learns from my yin.

Recently I dreamed that Mark and I confronted the head of a man which was alive, though bodiless. We sensed that he was evil, and our suspicions were confirmed by a letter from a friend which described the man's activities. Some were so terrible that they had been whited out, so as not to shock us. We sought sanctuary from this evil head by escaping to a large lake. Mark and I were in the water together; then we ascended into the sky, where I saw a hang glider off in the clouds. I wondered whether or not I should point it out to Mark—I knew he'd like to see it, but I didn't want to feed the obsession that already dominates too much of *our* life. (Last Christmas I wrestled with the decision to buy a hang-gliding calendar for Mark, who was already picking my patience to the bone with his endless chatter on the subject. Wouldn't it be just like giving a bottle of liquor to an alcoholic? In the end, I ordered the calendar. After all, it was the only item on his Christmas list!) I don't recall making a decision about the hang glider in the dream, whether or not to tell Mark about it. We floated back down to dry land, where we saw another live but bodiless head. This one was neither evil nor particularly good, but we knew he was harmless.

A dream head can symbolize a wide range of concepts, from wisdom to the cosmos and oneness. Because the focus of this dream is the hang glider, I have chosen the meaning of "attitudes" from Guiley's book, for the two heads. I have certainly felt hostility toward Mark's hang-gliding passion when it seems to detract too much from family time and finances. Then my attitude is extremely negative, although the evil dream head exaggerates my feelings to an extreme, perhaps as a warning that the consequences of my negativity could be evil, if I don't make the attempt to be more understanding.

Unlike the dream in which I rose up alone from the lake, in this dream Mark and I ascended together into the sky. Such an ascension from the unconscious to the heavens often symbolizes an initiation, an entry into a new phase of life, or the struggle that goes on during the process of change. I think that Mark and I are both struggling to preserve harmony in our marriage while pursuing our individual interests. In this dream I only managed to neutralize my "evil" attitude by considering the possibility of showing some interest in his passion. I don't know if I'll ever muster up any sincere enthusiasm for Mark's hang-gliding bug, but I *am* striving to tone my attitude to one of acceptance and neutrality.

Ascending together into the heavens, my husband and I agree that oneness with God is a goal we share. But why must he literally don wings like an angel to begin his quest? He makes fun of the altar I set up in front of a window, as if I were worshiping my blown-glass Madonna, a bouquet of flowers, and a candle. These are simple things that set the mood for my devotional times, and I don't have to drive to the top of a mountain to find them! Mark's method of finding inner peace requires a great deal of preparation, while I just like a holy setting for my meditations.

I might be content to contemplate God in my home and garden every day if it weren't for Mark and his exuberant drive to be busy all the time and preferably outside. I really am grateful to him for preventing me from leading the sedentary life I was heading for when we met in Yellowstone. Mark outfitted me with a friend's sleeping bag and his spare backpack so that I could camp out in the wilderness with him. As I trailed behind Mark, his hiking boots nimbly stepping over rocks and roots that tripped me as I scurried to keep up, I must have been attracted to his energy and daring. These same qualities have come to irritate me when they spill over into too many areas of my life, such as the back yard where he likes to pile and split logs, letting the chips spray all over the lawn that I care for. A neat lawn is merely pleasing to the eye, while splitting logs is exercise and a cost-effective means to heating our home. Compromise is an essential element in a balanced marriage, so Mark agreed to buy presplit logs and let me grow grass, and I agreed to the hang glider loan. Neither component of this compromise is cost effective, but each is essential to the happiness of one of us.

When we first met, I got Mark to read *Journeys Out of the Body*, a book by Robert A. Monroe that I found in the Yellowstone library. Mark knew about my fascination with unseen realms and mystical phenomena, but that didn't keep him from following me to Boston when the Yellowstone bar closed for the winter. Neither of us was a regular church attender before we met, but after we were married in my mother's church, we decided to make worship a regular part of our life together. Easter Sunday dawned one week after our wedding. We walked from our Somerville apartment to the bus stop, intending to go to the Cambridge Unitarian Church. While waiting for the bus and realizing we were going to be late for the service, we saw people going into a Congregational Church across the street. We attended the service there, and on the way out, when an usher asked if we were visitors, Mark replied, "We're Easter bigots." Of course, he meant to say "hypocrites," but either comment was embarrassing to me!

Now both of us have been elders in the Presbyterian Church, and Mark serves as a lay pulpit supply, occasionally filling in for absent preachers in local churches. While he doesn't understand my need to seek God in ways not necessarily sanctioned by the majority of churchgoers, Mark has frequently acknowledged that his faith would probably still be in the seed stage if I hadn't watered it and coaxed it along. The last time Mark preached, he used some examples from Catherine Marshall's and Mother Teresa's books, and told the congregation, "My wife is the reader in the family. She points out the good parts, and I share them with you."

I hope that, as Mark and I partake more of the nutritious bread that Christ bakes for us, we will be so filled with its good ingredients—patience, kindness, generosity, forgiveness, and the ability to "bear all things"—that we will actually rejoice in our differences, which, after all, brought us together in the first place. Meanwhile, our dream swims and our joint ascent into the clouds are encouragement for our struggle. And I am looking forward to Christmas morning this year, when Mark will open the hang-gliding windsock I bought for him!

1. Guiley, p. 338.

16

To Be Content
Bottles and Boats on the Harbor

When I sought advice from a career counselor in 1990, she suggested that I read *Women of Power*, by Laurel King, for inspiration. Mark gave me the book for Christmas, and I read with fascination the stories of ten extraordinary women and their secrets of success. Among the women portrayed in this book are Virginia Satir, M.A., D.S.S., known as the "Columbus of Family Therapy"; Anne Wilson Schaef, Ph.D., internationally known for her groundbreaking books on addictions and codependence; and Elisabeth Kübler-Ross, M.D., a world-renowned author, psychiatrist, and humanitarian. I guess the counselor was insinuating that I should set my sights higher than the part-time job I told her I needed to supplement our family income. As I read the life stories of these remarkable women, I received the distinct impression that an extraordinary life and a life committed to husband and family are not compatible. I think there was one exception to that rule among the women portrayed in the book—and, of course, there have been numerous exceptions throughout history. However, to be committed to husband and family *and* be a "woman of power" in the world must require something bordering on supernatural abilities.

My idea of a successful, if not extraordinary, life is one in which all of the essential elements of life work together. For me, these include family and friends; time to meditate and be alone with God; time to exercise; time to keep my home in order; time to write; time to make contributions to the welfare of my church, my community, and the world in which I live; and time to be alone with my thoughts while gardening, reading, or just doing nothing at all. I know that there are women who rise at four or five o'clock in the morning in order to meditate, write, or do housework before their families get up, and there are others who stay up until midnight, their energy never flagging. Still others have chosen a different set of essential elements—perhaps fewer—so that they can concentrate on one major goal and achieve great things, one after another. If I don't get eight hours of sleep and a little quiet time each day, I get very grumpy, and Mark starts to recite one of his pet refrains: "I want you to be happy!"

Paramahansa Yogananda said, "Success lies in learning the art of inner contentment: Acquire what you need, and then be satisfied with what you have."[1] Usually I am content with life as it is, and when I become restless and dissatisfied, the Dream Weaver gently reminds me to stay on the path I'm on. Or not so gently, as in the following dream that started out beautifully and ended up as a nightmare. It came to me in the fall of 1997 when the idea for this book was germinating, and Mark's decision to buy a hang glider was rekindling those old "part-time job" proddings. It began with an intuitive exercise I was doing with another woman, similar to what I had done at a spirituality workshop. We sat opposite each other, cross-legged on the floor, eyes closed, waiting for an image or symbol to appear in our minds. I saw a candle burning in a golden candlestick composed of many linked rings. I described it to the other woman, and she said she saw a white horse. "Oh, I saw a white horse, too!" I responded.

Then, I was part of a group of people, and one said to me, "It is very significant that you should be here at this time. This is the only time that this man has been here, and he has the ability to see auras."

In the next scene I recall that I was looking at a map, figuring out how to get home to Mark across a narrow body of water. While crossing the water, I was threatened by a shark. Next I witnessed a horrible scene between a father and a son: the father was slashing at the boy with a razor. Finally the boy stabbed the father in the belly with a spear. The father died, and I awoke, trembling.

I have spent a lot of time trying to piece this dream together. Some of the pieces will probably never make sense. But, when I first woke up, the phrase, "It is very significant that you should be here at this time," reverberated in my consciousness loud and clear above the more obscure images. The phrase said to me that I was in a good place on my life's path and that I should continue in the direction I was heading.

A lighted candle symbolizes divine light. The golden rings on the candlestick remind me of wedding bands, symbolizing the eternal love and fidelity of marriage, but also the never-ending love of God. The linked rings could represent the many aspects of love which I experience in my life, both familial and divine, that keep my spiritual light burning.

What of the white horse? Edgar Cayce said that the white horse instructs us to master, balance, and control the creative energy that flows from our reproductive glands, transforming it into the fuel that kindles genius, love, and extrasensory perception. Elsie Sechrist described them as "the crowns of life enabling the person to better serve."[2] Combined with the candle image and the message about being in the right place, I feel that the white horse image confirms that I am using my spiritual light to express the Divine Source within me, and I am attaining a greater balance of creative energy through the writing and other work I've been doing.

Dream fathers are often authority figures who may criticize and condemn. The father who slashed at his son probably represents my own critical nature, the part of me that inhibits my creative energy with fear and doubt. "Stop flagellating yourself for doing what you want to do!" the Dream Weaver is saying. The boy must be my creative self who slays the doubter and claims victory. So the nightmarish end to my dream is actually symbolic of triumph when examined closely.

The journey homeward to Mark, security, and family took up a large portion of the dream, although I don't recall many details. Crossing the shark-infested river, I seemed to be leaving one phase of life for another, even though it meant a return to the place from where I'd come. I had probably drifted from home in my ponderings about jobs that would take me away from hearth, loved ones, and writing desk. Yes, I know I would have returned home every day from the college teaching position for which I applied, but my spare time would have been consumed with chores and errands, and this book would not have been written. The shark who threatened me with its razorlike teeth emphasized the message of the angry father who tried to subdue his son with violence. I do violence to myself when I ignore the still, small voice that whispers, "Be content with who and what you are."

The urgency I felt about getting back to Mark, despite tremendous obstacles, highlights my commitment to my marriage as an essential ingredient in my creative life. While most of those "women of power" had to divorce their husbands in order to discover their full potential, remaining linked to Mark enables me to lead the balanced kind of life that is most fulfilling for me. True, I spend more time on housework and laundry than I had planned to when I envisioned my "marriage of equality" so many years ago. But then I had no concept of the many tasks that keep a marriage and a home functioning smoothly. Mark and I both contribute time and energy to the maintenance of our family life, and our contributions fit together like the individual elements of a painting.

Sometimes we dabble in colors that clash or one of us may accidentally undo the work of the other on one section of the painting. But we strive for overall harmony in this ever-changing picture, the subject of which, of course, is the city of peace from that long-ago dream. As we struggle to maintain balance in the various elements of this painting, I like to remind myself of some advice to married couples given by Edgar Cayce:

> In the establishing of the home, make it as that which may be the pattern of a heavenly home. Not as that set aside for only a place to sleep or to rest, but where not only self but all who enters there may feel, may experience, by the very vibrations that are set up by each in the sacredness of the home, a helpfulness, a *hopefulness* in the air *about* the home . . . Make thine home, thine abode, [a place] where an angel would *desire* to visit, where an angel would seek to be a guest. 480-20

Any angels who have visited our home have been unseen guests, but I'm sure they drop by from time to time to offer guidance and encouragement, for the conflicts and disharmonies that occur in our family are never long-lasting and always forgiven, and how could this be, unless we are receiving divine assistance in response to our prayers and our flawed attempts at self-improvement?

A year prior to dreaming about the multilinked candlestick, I had a dream that assured me that Mark and I were making some gains in our attempts to improve our relationship. I saw myself choosing some new gold jewelry. Did I want a necklace or a pair of earrings? In the end, the only piece of jewelry I was wearing was a beautiful gold ring, wider and brighter than my little wedding band, and with a diamond in the center. It was on the ring finger of my left hand, and my wedding band was gone. I looked everywhere for the missing wedding ring, but couldn't find it.

When I awoke, I felt anxious about the symbolism of the missing wedding ring. Later that morning, in prayer, I saw the positive significance of the beautiful, more valuable ring taking its place. Just the day before that dream, I had been thinking that our marriage had reached a stage of greater harmony than Mark and I had previously managed. So the diamond ring blessed this new phase of marital harmony. Of course, that phase came before the hang-gliding conflict, but if we hadn't put so much work into building a strong marriage before the hang-glider landed in the middle of it, the walls of that city of peace would be crumbling even as I write.

The indestructible diamond is traditionally worn on engagement rings because it symbolizes purity and everlasting love. Guiley says, "Like the philosopher's stone of alchemy, the diamond also represents the union of opposites—of spirit and matter—that results in a wholeness of consciousness."[3] My dream diamond celebrates my marriage to Mark as one that unites two opposite temperaments, and it celebrates my ongoing attempt to unite the "matter" of everyday life with the divine spirituality in all of life. It is my partnership with Mark that enables me to invest so much effort and energy into this work, thus creating a home where we and our visitors experience a special feeling when we enter the door to our simple, yet cheerful blue-and-white kitchen.

I know other couples whose homes emanate this special, warm feeling. Some of these homes are clean and

SEEKING INFORMATION ON

holistic health, spirituality, dreams, intuition or ancient civilizations?
Call 1-800-723-1112, visit our Web site, or mail in this postage-paid card for a FREE catalog of books and membership information.

Name: _____

Address: _____

City: _____

State/Province: _____

Postal/Zip Code: _____ Country: _____

Association for Research and Enlightenment, Inc.
215 67th Street
Virginia Beach, VA 23451-2061

For faster service, call 1-800-723-1112.
www.edgarcayce.org

PBIN

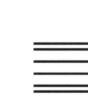

orderly; some are cluttered. But when I drop by to visit, I see evidence of creative activity: children's paintings on the walls, something savory baking in the kitchen, enticing books piled on an end table. The energy of love vibrates tangibly throughout the rooms. Most of these mothers have full-or part-time jobs in or out of the home. Sometimes, I think their lives are better structured than mine and their identities more clearly defined, because they have distinctive job titles. Comparing myself to others leads me back to that state of restlessness and dissatisfaction that denies the success of my simple life.

A few months after the Dream Weaver told me that I was in the *right* place, the part-time secretarial position at my church became open. What a nice environment to work in! I thought, and imagine getting paid, at least a little, for all the hours I would put in if I worked there! One of my church friends encouraged me to apply. I was tempted, but I knew it would mean giving up the four best hours of my day: the hours I spend meditating and writing before I start my "worldly" tasks. When the kids were home on vacation, though, I would still have to work. But wouldn't it be a good way to reenter the work force after being out of it for so many years? Back and forth went my thoughts until finally I decided to sleep on it.

I was at a "dream" vacation spot, showing my brother, Chris, a bed-and-breakfast where Mark and I had stayed earlier. Chris commented that the area looked pretty shabby. I hoped he would be more impressed when he saw the swimming pool. When we got there, it appeared that a wedding reception was taking place at the pool. Pink decorations were set up on the apron, and some floated on the water. From there, we went on to the motel where we planned to stay. Chris was in a suite with his wife, Gail, and my sister, Alyssa. I found myself in a suite with two people with whom I didn't think it would be as much fun to stay.

I had to go to the bathroom, which was occupied by another woman. While waiting my turn, I looked out of the window and gasped at the breathtaking scene I beheld. Snow-capped mountains towered above a boat-filled harbor. The woman came out and looked over my shoulder. She laughed and said, "That's not very pretty," because there were boat-sized cans and bottles floating on the water. To me, the scene was still beautiful.

I awoke from that dream feeling peaceful and content. I knew that the bed-and-breakfast represented a place where both Mark and I had enjoyed ourselves. My brother, who found it shabby, was looking at it from a different perspective—perhaps much the same way my life looks when I view it through someone else's eyes. Not long before this dream, my brother had told me that I am spoiled because I can stay home and write. I know he meant to say that I'm *lucky*, but I resented the comment, since it once was the norm for women to stay home, and their contributions to family and community were regarded as essential.

The bed-and-breakfast might symbolize the home where Mark and I are usually happy together and where the challenges of everyday life aid our spiritual growth. The color pink symbolizes love, joy, and happiness. Pink decorations graced the pool, where wedding rites and water symbolized an initiation into a new level of awareness. At this new level, I forego the opportunity to vacation with my fun-to-be-with siblings (and they are!) who in the context of this well-timed dream must have represented the good life I sometimes think I'm missing because I don't have that regular paycheck. I went to stay in the not-so-fun suite, as others may perceive my ordinary, stay-at-home life, and there I discovered a window with a beautiful view.

The boats that I saw beckoned me to continue my "voyage of life" toward those spiritual goals, which, as symbolized by towering mountains, are not easily attained. For some, a job in a church office would promise the opportunity to combine spiritual interests with useful work. But such a job would deny me the challenge of my writing career, usurp the quiet hours I need for spiritual renewal, and generate frenzy in the middle of the balanced life I have been striving so hard to achieve. The boat-sized soup cans and condiment bottles symbolized my everyday work: providing sustenance for my family. Their presence on the harbor was scoffed at by the woman who represented my critic, the one who listens to those who belittle the homemaker's job. But my true self saw how these homely symbols fit right into the beautiful picture: integral parts of my whole life's journey.

After I had that dream, I began to work on this book. Interweaving my dream life with my waking thoughts and experiences gave greater purpose to the plain and simple picture that is my life. When the new church secretary didn't work out, a friend begged me to put in an application. "I can't now," I told her. "I'm writing a book." That night I dreamed that I went back to college and told a fellow student, "I'm studying to be a better writer and a better gardener." At last, my true self and my dream self were in total agreement about who I really am.

During my real school years, I enjoyed being a nonconformist. I loved to tell people that a couple of football players and I played string bass in the high school orchestra. I was small and shy, so it was easy to shock my classmates by wearing a savage costume on Halloween or by railing out against cliques in English speech class. In college, I took outlandish courses that couldn't possibly have led to a traditional career. While my classmates were hallucinating on LSD, I went to the art studio and painted birds with human faces and multicolored dancers on a mountaintop, their arms raised toward a sky blazing with bursting stars. During those years of exploration, only the

Dream Weaver knew that I was destined to lead an ordinary life as a homemaker in the cozy home seen in my "empty paper bags" dream.

Recently, while I was getting dressed in the locker room after a swim at the YMCA, another swimmer asked me what kind of work I do. I told her that I write and that I stay home so I can take care of my family. "That's pretty unusual these days, isn't it?" she asked.

"Yes, I guess it is," I agreed. Wow! I thought to myself. Put that way, it sounds as if I'm the nonconformist I used to aspire to be, just by staying home and leading an ordinary life.

I mulled over this concept all the way home, feeling very pleased with myself.

◆ ◆ ◆

Contentment is an elusive feeling. It flutters in and out of my life like a bird looking for a nesting place. This year the bird of my soul has been happier with its nest than other years. Still, I know that the longevity of my contentment depends on my ability to maintain a balance of life's many elements, from green peppers and candy canes, to swimming and hang gliding. When a particular challenge or responsibility looms too large for my peace of mind, I'll seek serenity in the quiet breath of meditation and the imagery of my finer dreams.

A recurring theme in my dreams of contentment is a gently blowing breeze, which I liken to the breath of God. Not long after my dream of bottles and cans on the harbor, I had a lucid dream in which I found myself at a beach, symbol of a balance between earth and water or between head and heart. I was amazed by the vividness of the scene, of the sand and the waves, since I knew it was only a dream. Then I felt a soft wind blowing around me and I thought, "I can *really* feel the wind, even though this is just a dream!" The wind blew against my face in a steady rhythm. I started to breathe with the wind, slowly inhaling and exhaling, as I do in meditation. The wind and I breathed together, slowly in and out. We were one, the wind and I.

I awoke, filled with gratitude for the Dream Weaver's message: "What better symbol than this oneness with the breath of God, to confirm your need for contentment with life as it is?"

1. Paramahansa Yogananda, from talks given in October-November 1939. Self-Realization Fellowship, Golden Lotus Temple, Encinitas, Calif.
2. Sechrist, p. 185.
3. Guiley, p. 263.

EPILOGUE

Swimming Again
A New Birth

More than a year has passed since I wrote what I thought was the last chapter of this book. Much of it was typed left-handed, while my right arm hung in a sling around my neck. Early in January 1999, I went roller skating with my family, tripped over Mark's skate as his right foot pushed off in front of my left one, and I fell back onto my extended arm. My elbow was fractured and dislocated. Since I am right-handed, there was little I *could* do other than peck out words with my left hand.

As winter progressed into spring, and as family circumstances required that I seek employment, I realized that dislocating my elbow at the dawn of 1999 was a symbolic event for the "dislocation" that was taking place in my life. Looking back through my dream journal, I discovered a prophetic dream from July 1998, in which I went to a doctor because I was having trouble with my elbow! The doctor sat in bed, asking me questions: "If you weren't a writer, what would you want to do?"

"I don't know," I replied. "That's why I haven't chosen anything else."

"Many people don't have that luxury," he told me rather sternly. "They *have* to choose something." Then he asked if I had pictures of my children in my wallet as he did. "If you are interested in your children and in decorating your house, that shows that you are well-adjusted," he explained. This interview left me feeling deficient. The doctor's tone of voice made it obvious that he didn't think I *was* well-adjusted. As if that weren't bad enough, on the way out of the doctor's office, Mark told me that I should take a job teaching a subject I don't like (probably math!). I refused to consider it, so Mark was miffed, and the dream left me despondent.

When I received this dream, I did not realize that the Dream Weaver was preparing me for things to come: the dislocated elbow and the fact that I *would* have to choose some work other than writing. The material reason for this had to do with Mark's job situation and the increasing demands on our financial resources as Vera and Peter enter adolescence. The spiritual reason goes deeper. The lack of interest in my children referred to by the dream doctor did not imply that I'm an inadequate mother. Dream children symbolize unrealized potential, so the doctor was pointing out my need to acquire and develop new skills. If the house is the dwelling place of my soul, an interest in decorating it would imply a desire to embellish that eternal part of self with the results of the new skills I should acquire.

So, at the same time that I was dreaming and writing about contentment, an unrecognized part of myself saw a need to explore some of the new rooms I frequently discover in my dream houses. This is not necessarily a contradiction. One of Edgar Cayce's better known quotes is, ". . . be content; not satisfied . . ." (262-121) We can be content with our situation in life, and yet we should not be satisfied to stay there if we intend to grow and continue to learn new lessons. In my case, I may have been a bit too satisfied as well as content. Consequently, my husband (frequently the goad in my life) and the doctor (also symbolizing Mark, the healer, since he spoke to me from a bed, symbol of marriage) conspired to force me out of my complacency and into the work world, where I would learn lessons I thought I did not require.

Once it was determined that I had to obtain new skills and earn money, my daily prayer—"Send me, use me"—brought all kinds of opportunities into my life. I taught two sessions of a continuing education class for adults—*Writing from the Heart*—in the spring and the fall. I discovered that twenty years of writing practice, workshops, submissions, rejections, and published material provided me with a cache of wisdom and experience—pearls to share with aspiring writers. I told them that writing well requires courage. "It takes a willingness to let people see who we really are," I urged. Some of my students accepted this challenge and surprised themselves by producing some vivid and poignant pieces. Others tried to be cute and clever without revealing the contents of their hearts. Even so, each of us, students and teacher alike, experienced and produced something unique in those classes. The wheel of life may go round and round from generation to generation, but it moves forward, too. The teacher's bicycle is not stationary!

I earned a few hundred dollars from this venture, but still needed a regular income, so I took an introductory computer class during the summer. Computer skills are necessary for almost any kind of job these days, and mine were limited to the "antiquated" word processing program I'd been using for five years. In the class I learned the basics of Microsoft Office, and before the course was over, I had procured a part-time position as administrative assistant for the area Girl Scout office. So there I was, taking classes and working during the summer while my children were home, a way of life I had never wanted; but then, as the doctor in my dream reminded me, "Many people don't have that luxury."

◆ ◆ ◆

I worked in the reception area of a windowless suite in a large, windowless building. Each morning, when I traded the sun for fluorescent lights, I felt as if I were passing through the mouth of a deep, dark cave. My life had come full circle since the "empty paper bag" jobs of my young adult years. I typed recruitment flyers on the computer and fed sheet after sheet of paper into a printer that spat out all kinds of things totally unrelated to what I had just typed. Hundreds of copies had to be made on an ornery copier that jammed and crumpled more pages than the printer had ruined. I did use some of my new computer knowledge. At the same time that we were creating spreadsheets in my class, I was entering data about Girl Scouts on the same spreadsheet program in the office. And I got to use some of my writing skills to compose business letters for my boss, Janet, who had hired me largely for that purpose, writing not being her "forte."

In August, I had two dreams that confirmed I was where I should be, or at least that there were lessons to be learned in my current situation. In one of these dreams, I found myself attending a new college, and I realized that Janet was the one who had recruited me. I wondered what made that particular college better than others to which I might have gone. In the second dream, I was visiting our church office and saw Girl Scout signs on the walls. Why hadn't I realized that the church office and the Girl Scout office were one and the same?

There were lessons to be learned at this "college" job, but the church office symbolism suggested that there was also spiritual work for me to do in my new position. Perhaps the quirky office machines offered lessons in patience, but the most valuable opportunities arose from my daily interactions with volunteer leaders who came to me for badges and uniform pieces, information, and a sympathetic ear. These women ranged from doctors and teachers to Wal-Mart cashiers. They all shared a love for young girls and a desire to make a positive difference in their lives. I admired their ability to put in a full day's work and then go out and lead a Girl Scout meeting at night. I worked from four to five hours Monday through Wednesday, on Thursday nights, had Fridays off, and still I had trouble keeping up with errands, housework, and paperwork at home. By the time I had prepared supper, washed the pots and pans, and helped the kids with their homework, I felt as if I had put in a full day! (I had!) How did these women scrape up the energy to do so much more?

I thought I was just doing my job when I ordered the patches they needed, hounded the shop manager until she sent them from the council headquarters, and called the leaders as soon as their order was in. But their appreciation was so great that I soon realized my helpfulness was a gift I hadn't even considered when I'd listed the skills I could offer as an employee. When some of the leaders told Janet that they "loved" me, I was reminded of the time I bought gas at a convenience store, handed my money to the cashier, and thanked her for the change. "You're the nicest person I've met all day," she remarked, and I looked at her in astonishment. "But all I did was pay for my gas," I said. "Yes, but everyone else has been throwing money and cursing at me." Wow! The more people I meet, the more I discover that just being an ordinary, considerate person makes me a blessing to others.

When I interviewed for the Girl Scout job, Janet asked me if I could handle multiple tasks simultaneously. I told her I could do only one thing at a time, but that I knew how to prioritize what needed to be done first and that I was not easily flustered when several things happened at once. I knew what Janet meant about multiple tasks when I found myself totaling receipts for a bank deposit, then a volunteer came in looking for badges, and then the phone rang. I took a deep breath, picked up the receiver, and answered: "Girl Scouts, Indian Hills Council, where girls grow strong. This is Emily." It was like a centering prayer. By the time I had said all that, I was past the annoyance of the ringing phone, ready to concentrate on the needs of the caller.

In September I had another office dream. I was working as an administrative assistant for another company. I had been organizing other people's offices, but hadn't had time to take care of my own. I opened the door to my office and found that it was full of people, dressed like Hindus, who were performing a religious ritual. The office was decorated with Eastern Indian objects, including a small Buddha. I had two desks, just as I did at the Girl Scout office (one for the computer and one for other work). Perhaps the two dream desks stood for my new office work and my old writing work at home. I rummaged through the drawers in one of my dream desks and discovered a big bag of candles. I announced to the Hindus, "I suppose you've been using these for your rituals, but this is my desk now, and I don't want them in here." Of course, I planned to replace them with pens, pencils, tape, scissors, stamp pads, and other *useful* items.

Next, I looked around and noticed how large the office was and thought what fun it would be to decorate it. Perhaps I would keep some of the Indian theme so that I wouldn't have to change everything. But I don't like Indian art. I passed through a door into a connecting room, where most of the Hindus had gone, and announced rather pompously that this was *my* room and I was going to rearrange it to suit my taste. Then it occurred to me that it was not my room—after all, I was only the administrative assistant. "Never mind," I said and went back to the office.

These realizations, that the second room was not mine to rearrange and the fact that I'd been busy organizing other people's offices, reminded me that, while I could be a channel of blessings for others at the Girl Scout office, it was not a vocation to which I truly belonged. It was not the place of which theologian Frederick Buechner spoke when he said, "The place God calls you to is the place where your deep gladness and the world's deep hunger meet." On one level, I realized that my knack for creating order out of chaos will always be a welcome gift in an office setting, and I do gain a sense of satisfaction when I have organized a mess. On a deeper level, I felt frustrated because I was not using what I consider to be my higher gifts of creativity and spiritual insight. And the meager remuneration I received for my efforts made me feel like the "me" in my dream who said, "Never mind . . ." (Who do I think I am anyway? I'm just a cog in this organization.)

In the days before I took a job, most mornings I set aside some time for devotional reading, prayer, and meditation after the children had gone to school. Sometimes I'd light a candle to magnify the holy hush of the hour. Sometimes I kept the candle burning as I went to work, composing prose on my computer. Now the dream "me" wanted to get rid of the bag of candles in my desk drawer. I had no place for them in my new life. The very thing I had feared when considering the church office job a year earlier had occurred. The quiet hours I needed for spiritual renewal had been usurped, and frenzy had been generated in the middle of what had been, if briefly, a balanced life.

The Dream Weaver was warning me that I was in danger of losing my ability to integrate the sacred into my everyday life and work. The pompous attitude of the dream "me" paralleled my conscious feeling that, if I had to work for money, I might as well set my sights on a better job. I wanted a position where I would use more of my creative talents, get paid a professional salary, and have my own office—not the reception area for someone else's office. But wouldn't such a position make it even more difficult to keep my commitments to family and to God?

I knew that I could never be like my supervisor, Janet, or like Bobbie, who also worked in our office. Both women have children younger than mine, put in many more hours of work for the Girl Scout council's goals, and also own catering businesses, for which they work on their days off. They are the kind of women who thrive on constant activity and interaction with people. Bobbie often talked about how bored she would be if she weren't employed: "I get up at 5:30, clean the house, and make breakfast for the boys. My house is so clean by 10:00 in the morning, you could eat off my floor. What would I do if I stayed home? Sit around and drink cocktails all day?"

If anyone ate off *my* floor, she'd get a spoonful of dust and dog hair with every bite (unless it happened to be the day after my annual scrub and wax). Cleaning is just as boring to me as addressing envelopes to scores of Girl Scout leaders. Still, when I stayed home, it was a major effort to find time to "sit around." I made that effort, though, because, if I don't spend large doses of time alone, in inspirational reading, writing, and intro-spection, I find myself out of balance. Consequently I'm out-of-sorts, like the haughty person I was in the dream when I spoke rudely to the Hindus in my office.

About the time that I had this dream, I read Robert Johnson's book, *Balancing Heaven and Earth: A Memoir of Visions, Dreams, and Realizations*, in which he says that the cross symbolizes the balanced life. The horizontal beam represents the earthly or "doing" nature, and the vertical beam is the heavenly or "being" nature. Each of us has a different point of balance, requiring different amounts of "doingness" and "beingness." Bobbie and Janet are the kind of women whose point of balance is much closer to the earth than mine, which is way up in the mesosphere somewhere. The Dream Weaver was showing me the kind of person I could turn into if I tried to move my point of balance closer to the earth.

◆ ◆ ◆

All the while I was teaching, job hunting, and learning computer skills, my book proposal was making the rounds of editors and agents and coming back rejected. The same day that I was offered the Girl Scout job, an agent requested the complete manuscript and sent me a six-month contract for a fee of $150 to cover copying costs and postage. I decided to take the risk, since I'd be too busy to keep sending out proposals myself. I felt that, even if this agent were unsuccessful, the year I'd spent on the book had not been wasted. The process of writing it had helped me to make sense of my life, up to the time I dislocated my elbow, and had prepared me for the many changes I was undergoing. Somehow, the knowledge that I had successfully completed a book sustained me during the long detour away from my writing life. July was the real turning point for me during this transitional year. I recorded very few dreams that month, whether because I didn't remember them or because I was too busy adjusting to my new lifestyle, I don't know. Besides taking the computer class, signing the agent's contract, and starting my job that month, it was July when I met Lesley.

Lesley is the executive director for Catskill Area Hospice and Palliative Care, Inc. Prior to this time, my knowledge of hospice was all indirect. A friend of Mark's had been the chaplain there; I knew people who volunteered for hospice; and we had a church friend whose wife had been cared for by hospice when she was dying. We had contributed money in her name, so we were on the mailing list for the hospice newsletter, *Sharing the Spirit*. When this newsletter arrived last summer, my inner guidance spoke to me, a lot louder than usual. One of the messages it relayed was that Catskill Area Hospice is a place where spiritual work is done, the kind of place where I might like to work someday. The second message was a reminder that hospice was largely responsible for my little successes in the publishing world over the last six years, and it had never occurred to me to thank them.

In the fall of 1993, when I was just beginning to experiment with creative nonfiction, Mark and I attended a lecture by Tom Sawyer (coauthor with Sydney Farr of *What Tom Sawyer Learned from Dying*), which was sponsored by the Catskill Area Hospice. Sawyer spoke about his near-death experience (NDE), during which he encountered the unconditional love of Christ and witnessed his entire life in review, not only as it had happened to him, but from the viewpoint of everyone else who had been a part of his life. While I had read Dr. Raymond A. Moody, Jr.'s book, *Life After Life*, and a few other stories about NDEs, I didn't recall any previous knowledge of the life review. This concept raised some provocative questions for me, which I presented in an article that I submitted to *Venture Inward*, the member magazine of the A.R.E.

Thanks to those clever angels who like to work behind the scenes, editor Bob Smith had just received a review copy of the book, *What Tom Sawyer Learned from Dying*. He called me while I was sorting laundry and asked if I was busy. (As if I wouldn't welcome an interruption by a magazine editor!) "How would you like to read this book and then turn your article into a book review?" Bob asked. He was offering to pay me to do something *fun*. The review was published in the July/August 1994 issue of *Venture Inward*. It was the first of many reviews and several articles that I would write for Bob. His confidence in my work encouraged me to continue writing and submitting articles and essays to other magazines, as well as to *Venture Inward.*

I put this story in a letter to Catskill Area Hospice and Palliative Care, Inc., along with a copy of my article: "Life Review Revealed in Near-Death Experience." Several days later, right after my second interview for the Girl Scout office job, I received a phone call from Lesley, thanking me for my letter and article. It turned out that it had been her idea to invite Tom Sawyer to speak in Oneonta. She had received some criticism for this decision from the fundamentalists in our community, so she was pleased to read a positive response to the event.

Sensing a sympathetic spirit in one another, we conversed at length about life after life and the recent death of Lesley's adult son. She described for me the profound experience of washing his body to prepare it for burial. I told her about my transition from at-home mom and writer to employment seeker. She asked if I had ever considered grant writing as a line of work, and I replied that the possibility had crossed my mind. I knew very little about the process, but I was willing to learn. It turned out that the hospice development coordinator and grant writer had just given her notice, and the next thing I knew, I was getting dressed to interview for the job!

Meeting Lesley was one of those cosmic occurences that we all experience at rare moments. Divine order and purpose were as tangible as the heat in her office that sultry afternoon. We both interpreted this to mean that I should take the position of development coordinator. It was a full-time job, requiring expertise in marketing and business management. The idea of diving into such a demanding position was intimidating, but the synchronicity of events plus Lesley's persuasive skills nearly pushed me off the springboard. Hadn't I always felt I was capable of doing greater things, if only the opportunity would present itself? But was I really ready for such a *big* opportunity? Before I left her office, Lesley said to me,

"Sometimes God's timing is different from ours."

Janet offered me the Girl Scout office assistant job. While I was wrestling with my decision between a light schedule with low pay and a challenging job with better pay and too many hours, I had the following dream: I was lying in bed while a woman, a nurse, watched over me. She said it made her sleepy to watch me sleep! I stayed in bed, because it was so dark out that I assumed it was night. Then I looked at my clock and saw that it was 9:00 a.m., so I got up and went outside. The sky was a predawn gray. Someone told me there had been a disaster in New York City that had created a lot of dust that was blocking the sun. My thought was that this was one of the planetary disasters that had been predicted for the new millennium. I got down on my knees, bowed my head to the ground, and prayed.

In the beginning of this dream, I slept right through a major disaster. Planetary disaster, in dreams, denotes the possibility of major changes in one's life, of things coming apart. By sleeping through this warning, I demonstrated my lack of foresight regarding a job that would turn my life upside down. The nurse could have been Lesley, who *was* a nurse before she took on her first administrative role at hospice. Nurses can symbolize the dreamer's desire to be taken care of. I wanted to put my destiny in Lesley's hands, but she grew sleepy watching me sleep—she, too, was unaware of pending disaster!

When I awoke from that dream, I continued to pray: for guidance, for my highest good, for the good of my family and those I'd be serving in whatever job I chose. I placed the decision in God's hands and He made it for me, via the wisdom of Lola, clinical director for hospice, who told Lesley I was not qualified for the position of development coordinator. I was surprised by the extent of my relief when Lesley relayed this news to me: I felt the tension wash out of my body as if a cleansing shower was pouring through me. Still, I think Lesley and I were both disappointed. "I know we met for a reason," she said. "Someday we'll know what it is."

◆ ◆ ◆

More than three months passed before I spoke to Lesley again. During that time I worked at the Girl Scout office, taught the fall writing class, took the kids to doctor's appointments, watched Peter's soccer games, smoothed out some of the bumps in Vera's middle school experience, and tried to keep all of my batons in the air at once. In October, I took a single-session grant-writing class, thinking that the knowledge might eventually lead to a better job opportunity. From time to time, I thought about Catskill Area Hospice, how a job there would have been more interesting than my office work, and how it would have been so much more time consuming.

Then, as I was driving one Friday to the Community Education building to photocopy materials for my class, I wondered how Lesley was doing, whether she was still struggling with grief for her son, and whether she was managing all of her responsibilities in spite of it. I decided to call her when I got home and tell her about Robert Johnson's cross analogy.

My phone call was timely, because the first anniversary of the death of Lesley's son was approaching, and the knowledge that others were thinking of her was heartening. She liked the reminder to keep her life balanced between heaven and earth. That's an enormous challenge for someone with the responsibilities and emotional burdens of a hospice director, but she's the kind of person who really needs more of that quiet time with God to balance the hectic pace of her work life. After we had talked for a while, Lesley suggested that we meet for lunch sometime. It turned out that she never did fill the position for a development coordinator, and she thought I might be able to help out with the grant-writing part of the job.

When Lesley gave me two file folders of material that I'd need to write my first grant letters, I accepted them as if they were a gift. "I appreciate the opportunity to do a new thing!" I told her. Lesley let me use her office while she went out to a meeting, so I sat at her computer, arranging ideas and words thinking, "Hey, this is fun!" I had never said that to myself while working in the Girl Scout office. Not only was I enjoying the work, but Lesley was paying me three times my current hourly wage. I felt like a professional, because someone recognized that I had valuable skills to share.

Lesley was pleased with my first two grant letters, so she asked me to continue as the regular hospice grant writer. When I'd first set out to procure a part-time job, I had planned to spend some of my "free" time in creative writing. But the computer class, then my writing class, and now the grant writing filled those spare hours, and I was so preoccupied with my pursuit of new opportunities that I had neither the time nor the inclination to write anything other than my journal entries. In January I added a morning tutoring job to my schedule. All of these opportunities to gain new experiences and earn money must have been manifesting for a purpose, I thought. How could I turn one down? The tutoring might be another key to a future beyond routine office work!

◆ ◆ ◆

One Saturday morning in mid-January, I awoke early and wrote in my journal:

> Everyone else is still asleep. I've been lying in bed awake, thinking how different my life is from what it used to be. Sometime during the night, it

occurred to me that, while I wrote a book on accepting an ordinary life as a homemaker, my life is much more ordinary now that I'm employed. This last week, I tutored and worked on a grant, in addition to my Girl Scout office work. Full-time hours, except that a snow storm on Thursday gave me a reprieve from tutoring and Girl Scouts. I have to work most of the time I'm home to keep up with laundry, shopping, bills, and *some* cleaning. So, I've become a typical, modern-day woman. When I spent time in the mornings meditating and writing and occasionally seeing something I'd written in print, my life was not ordinary, but unique. Of course, there were low points, especially rejection days and doubting days. But the highs were sweeter than what I experience in an ordinary work life.

Friday, Mark was excited to learn that he'd received a three percent raise. Yesterday I revised the monthly budget accordingly and discovered that most of the excess would be needed to pay for Vera's orthodontics and other cost-of-living increases. So, my need for a regular income is real and permanent.

The week of that journal entry, the contract period with my literary agent ran out. She said she still had several markets in mind, so would I consider renewing for another $150? No, I was using my extra income to pay off a loan for the driveway we had paved in the fall, and I was determined not to follow in the footsteps of writers like Robert L. Pirsig who sent *Zen and the Art of Motorcycle Maintenance* to 116 publishers before it was accepted. There was a limit to the amount of rejection I could take! Sure, it would be nice to get my book published, but maybe I'd be just as happy if I found a new part-time job where I could combine my grant-writing skills with some of my other capabilities. Or wouldn't someone hire me to tend their gardens, give them Reiki, and interpret their dreams?

Before I gave up on my book altogether, I decided I would send a proposal to the A.R.E. Press. I knew it was a long shot, because several years earlier Joe Dunn of A.R.E. Press had written to inform me that he wasn't accepting autobiographical work such as my writing tends to be. Still, I felt I should make one last attempt to sell my manuscript before filing it away with the other items in my archives labeled: "You haven't done anything if you haven't failed."

After making this decision, I had the following dream:

> I flew under my own power to a tiny island in order to retrieve a pattern for a cloak I was going to sew for myself. Broken arrows lay scattered over the beach. My enemies, a man and a boy, were ready to attack me. "You wouldn't shoot me when I'm weaponless, would you?" I pleaded, as I flew away again. My hands were full, so I couldn't carry *my* bow and arrows. It was late—nearly 10 o'clock—so I headed for home. But I planned to return to that island where my enemies awaited me, when my cloak was ready to wear.

Broken arrows usually represent broken vows or broken plans. At this point in my life, my plans to be a writer seemed to be shattered. My island enemies symbolized the circumstances that had broken the arrows: my vows to be content as a homemaker and writer. The island, small and barren, was isolated from the familiar world as was the windowless Girl Scout office, where routine duties sabotaged my creativity. I made a plea to my enemies, thinking, if they'd just give me a little time, I could return wearing my cloak and carrying my bow and arrows.

My dream encyclopedia tells me that a cloak is a garment that would disguise my true nature or render me invisible. I can't make this meaning fit the context of my life, and "pattern" isn't in the dream encyclopedia, so I looked it up in *The American Heritage Dictionary,* where I found the definition: "ideal worthy of imitation." *A Search for God, Book 1,* says, "The true ideal is the highest spiritual attainment to be reached on this material plane; hence, it follows that our ideal must be found in Christ, who is the Way."[1] Edgar Cayce also spoke of Jesus' life as the *pattern* after which we should order our own lives. If the cloak pattern is a symbol for the Christ, the cloak may very well represent the seamless garment for which the soldiers cast lots after hanging Jesus on the cross. According to the *Metaphysical Bible Dictionary,* this cloak represents spiritual Truth in its "harmonious expression and unchangeable perfection."[2]

It makes sense that, if I were to retrieve the pattern that the Christ established for my life and put on the cloak of Truth, I would be invincible against any adversarial circumstances that would keep me from my highest good. The Truth that I needed to secure my salvation was the knowledge that I am not identified by my occupation, but by the fact that I am a child of God. As God's child, I live by faith, knowing that each step of my life's journey and each job I take make up the part of God's plan that I am.

It was 10 o'clock at night when my dream self realized that I had to go home to work on my cloak. The number ten has several significant meanings. For this dream, I have chosen the symbolism of completion and a return to origins: ten equals one plus zero which equals one. I had learned my necessary lessons at the Girl Scout office, and while I didn't know it yet, my book proposal would be accepted by A.R.E. Press, an event that would reestablish my identity and confidence as a writer.

Throughout this dream I remained in the air, first hovering above the island as I reached down to fetch my pattern, then taking flight to escape from my enemies. Flying in a dream usually symbolizes inspiration and means that one is not stuck or limited. It also signals a readiness to act and make changes. When this dream came to me, I thought that I had made too many changes already. There I was, scraping snow from my car so that I could scuttle from one job to another to another. I didn't have time to sit down and revise my book proposal to fit the A.R.E. guidelines. Still, I caught a hint of a promise in this dream. Perhaps there were changes ahead of which I wasn't yet aware. The next night, I dreamed that I received two job promotions in one day. Surely something was going on back in the wings, off the stage of life, beyond my scope.

◆ ◆ ◆

A couple of weeks later, there was a lull in the tutoring and grant-writing opportunities, so I prepared my book proposal on a Friday and mailed it to the A.R.E. Just that little bit of writing reminded me how much I enjoy that kind of work, and how much I missed it. But the infrequent checks I received from my writing efforts didn't pay many bills. The changes and the job promotions I'd dreamed about must foretell a new and better job opportunity for which I'd better be preparing. I searched the want ads, hoping to find one good position to take the place of the three jobs that were fragmenting my life.

Writing grant letters at hospice was still my favorite job, but too sporadic to be my only job. I was sitting at Lesley's computer one snowy morning when a friend called to invite me to a spirituality workshop at her church that Saturday. The promise of that retreat pulled me through the remainder of a week that closed a frazzling month in which

I'd maneuvered around several major snowstorms to various destinations. These included a funeral for one of Vera's classmates, plus several trips to the hospital where Vera stayed when a stomach virus left her severely dehydrated. I was delighted to leave the laundry and the dirty house with Mark and the kids so that I could walk a masking-tape labyrinth on the floor of the Unitarian Universalist Church.

I chose a journaling workshop for the morning session. The woman who conducted it was a counselor and dream consultant. She led us through several writing assignments designed to call forth our inner guidance. One of these was a dialogue that began with a question to an imagined mentor. Then we wrote down the imagined answer, and so it went. I recorded my question: "Can I find work that is both joyful to do and results in abundance for me and my family?"

My inner mentor, whom I named Babette, tried to convince me that I could find joy in my work, whatever it might be. I argued that I wasn't saintly enough to manage that Buddha-like joy in mundane tasks on a regular basis. "You don't have to be a saint," Babette insisted. "But you can be patient and loving in your connections with Girl Scout leaders and co-workers, as well as with your family members. Remember this day, your daily bread. Your needs are met each day. Accept them joyfully, and tomorrow's bread may be tastier and more nutritious."

"Okay," I relented, "but if I partake of today's bread joyfully, what happens to the decision making, the inner conflict I'm struggling with regarding my future? I have to decide whether or not to apply for a new job or to pursue grant writing as a profession. I have to take concrete steps or my opportunities will be lost."

Babette had the final word: "Cease the inner struggle and clarity will come. Decisions are hardly even necessary when we are patient and allow circumstances to choose for us. You've seen this happen in your life many times before—after needless anxiety. This time, relax, and everything will fall into place much more easily."

Then it was time for lunch, the labyrinth, and a lesson on the Enneagram, which divides people into head, heart, and gut personalities. (I'm a head person, for sure, concerned with connections and patterns in life, always asking: Where am I? What is happening to me?) I left for home before the closing ceremony—too many hours cloistered in a building with stained-glass windows and fluorescent lights had given me a headache. (Head people are prone to headaches.) There, in the pile of bills and catalogues on my desk, was a letter from Brenda English, an editor at A.R.E. Press, expressing interest in my book.

I had to read the letter three times before I could convince myself that the A.R.E. editors were *seriously* interested in my book. I have received countless letters from editors who say they like my work *but* . . . There was no big "but" in this letter—just some requests for minor revisions which were easily made in a couple of days. Then, there was a long period of waiting—waiting for the editors to read my complete manuscript, waiting for the contract to be drawn up, waiting to see if this change in my life's circumstances was part of the answer to the question I'd posed for my imaginary mentor. While I waited, I continued to perform my duties at the Girl Scout office four days a week. Boxes and boxes of cookies had to be receipted in and out of the office each day, and hundreds of badges and pins counted and sold. I asked to have my name removed from the tutoring list after two "special needs" boys proved to me that teaching those who have no interest in learning is not one of my gifts. I still wondered if there was a better job "somewhere out there," where I could use the gifts I do have. A few nights after I received Brenda's letter, I dreamed that Janet was giving me some instructions over the phone. My father drove up in a car and stopped in front of me. The car was filling up with muddy water. "Can I go now?" I asked Janet. The water was rising fast. I had to get Dad out of the car right away. "I have to go!" I shouted to Janet and hung up the receiver.

Clearly, the time to leave my job was approaching. Not yet, because spring is the busiest season on the Girl Scout calendar, and I didn't have a way to compensate for the loss of income. But dream fathers sometimes symbolize willpower and ambition, and I saw that letting my loyalty to Janet and Bobbie overpower my need to follow my own ambitions could drown that aspect of myself. To be submerged in dream water indicates dissolution of the old and birth of the new. Mud germinates new life, such as ideas and creativity. So the muddy water symbolized an opportunity for a new, more creative life when I was ready to tell Janet, "I have to go!"

In mid-March Brenda told me that she liked my completed manuscript, although she'd probably want me to add to it. The following Thursday afternoon, I had planned to attend a class on finding the hidden job market. In the morning, I indulged in a longer-than-usual meditation period. Then, as I busied myself with chores— vacuuming, grocery shopping, baking brownies for Peter to take to school for his birthday the next day—the full significance of having my book accepted for publication finally dawned on me. This was a divine gift, an affirmation that writing is my true calling. Why should I be spending time and energy looking for a job when I could be writing? I didn't go to the class, and the following Thursday and Friday I sat down and wrote an article, the first one I'd written in many months.

In mid-April I received the contract. The publishers were requesting that I add to my book—the more the better! The final manuscript was due by the end of the summer. I have never been able to write very much during summers when the kids are home from school, and there is a lot of visiting back and forth with relatives.

My personal goal was to finish all or most of the book by the time school let out at the end of June. I didn't know if I could manage it while continuing to work at the Girl Scout office. Was this the time to leave? Janet and Bobbie were overwhelmed with demands on their time and energy. I felt guilty about creating extra work for them. And what about the loss of income? The advance would be enough to replace my paycheck for a few months, and I had several grant letters to write in May. Perhaps I could find another job in the fall, or perhaps a way would open for me to write another book.

I went to bed that night with all of these thoughts and questions tumbling around in my head. I dreamed that I was taking a trip with my family, first to go sightseeing in New York City, then to swim at a Girl Scout camp. Reassessing this plan, I realized that sightseeing in the city is enough activity for one day. Later, we'd be going to a pretty park in upstate New York, and we could swim there. Why did I think we had to squeeze in a trip to the Girl Scout camp near the city just because I worked for the Girl Scouts? It occurred to me that the camp was available for people who lived in the city and who didn't have the opportunity to visit a rural park, which would be prettier and quieter.

This dream expedited my decision to resign from my Girl Scout position. There is so much to see and do in New York City that, the one day my family really did spend there, we had only a little peek at the Metropolitan Museum of Art and a few other "wonders" before we had to catch the bus home. I think the Dream Weaver was comparing that kind of busyness with my current sched-ule, packed as it is with writing, grant-writing deadlines, and family activities that seem to require my chauffeuring services several times a day! Enough is enough, and I shouldn't feel obligated to "swim" with the Girl Scouts when I could be replaced by someone else who likes that hectic "city pace." The pretty, rural park where we'll later go to swim reminds me that my future is in God's hands. When I've finished this book and the money has been spent, God will show me the next step. After all, swimming represents the spiritual birth of a new self.

I gave Janet a month's notice, so that I could help out in the office until most of the cookie money was collected and she would have time to procure a new administrative assistant. When the right person accepted the job, I took that as further confirmation that my decision was part of God's plan, since a divine plan has to work out for everyone involved. Still, during my last days in the Girl Scout office, I frequently questioned the wisdom of my decision. Part-time jobs are scarce in this small, rural city, and last year's experiences had proved to me that I couldn't handle full-time work. What if I couldn't find another job? Every time I asked myself that question, I remembered my dream guidance and my faith that God would lead me to that beautiful place "Where my deep gladness and the world's hunger meet."

So I have returned to my "old" life as writer and homemaker, the life with which I had learned to be content before my foray into the workaday world. But we never really return to an old phase of life. I continue to write grant letters for Lesley, so I keep one foot in the world of employment, realizing that I may yet return there in another capacity. I am finishing my first-to-be-published book, and so my view of myself as a writer is more secure than it was before my long sabbatical from that occupation. My children, now deeply embroiled in rebellious adolescence, remind me that, in too few years, my services as a mother will no longer be required—all the more reason to keep open my options for other occupations. And I have learned that, while it is always good to be content with present circumstances, I should not be so satisfied that I overlook opportunities for new and different experiences.

Since the dislocation of my elbow a year and a half ago, I have done more "new" things than I could possibly squeeze into this epilogue. Much of the time I felt discouraged because I wasn't happy about all of these new things, and didn't see where they were leading me. Throughout these experiences, I kept my journal and documented my most vivid dreams. Now I can look back, interweave the stories from my journal and my dream diary, and find meaning and purpose in much of what has happened in my life. I think keeping these journals is a way of demonstrating my faith. When I first record the events of a day or the dreams from the night before, I may see very little meaning in what I write. Yet I know that the day will come when much of it will fall together and speak to me like a message from the Holy Spirit.

One of the messages that comes through my dream journals—as I discover dream after dream about birth, death, an ascent into the sky, a transit over a bridge, swimming, and other symbols of initiation and new life—is that life renews itself over and over, and spiritual growth is a never-ending process. Whether a dream encourages contentment with the present or promises a new and exciting stage of life, I will know that this does not indicate the end of my life's quest. If still another dream suggests that I'm backsliding into complacency or imbalance, I'll know that it's not an ultimatum, but a gentle hint that it's time again for renewal. Dreams are among the many guideposts that God gives us to direct our paths on the journey of life. As with any guideposts, it takes faith to follow them, even when we don't know what we'll find around the next bend or up the hill. There is one thing I'm certain of, though: Each night presents me with another dream.

1. *A Search for God, Book i*, p. 38.
2. *Metaphysical Bible Dictionary*, Unity School of Christianity, Unity Village, Mo., 1931, p. 153.

A.R.E. Press

The A.R.E. Press publishes quality books, videos, and audio-tapes meant to improve the quality of our readers' lives—personally, professionally, and spiritually. We hope our products support your endeavors to realize your career potential, to enhance your relationships, to improve your health, and to encourage you to make the changes necessary to live a loving, joyful, and fulfilling life.

For more information or to receive a free catalog, call:

1-800-723-1112

Or write:

A.R.E. Press
215 67th Street
Virginia Beach, VA 23451-2061

Discover How the Edgar Cayce Material Can Help You!

The Association For Research and Enlightenment, Inc. (A.R.E.®), was founded in 1931 by Edgar Cayce. Its international headquarters are in Virginia Beach, Virginia, where thousands of visitors come year round. Many more are helped and inspired by A.R.E.'s local activities in their own hometowns or by contact via mail (and now the Internet!) with A.R.E. headquarters.

People from all walks of life, all around the world, have discovered meaningful and life-transforming insights in the A.R.E. programs and materials, which focus on such areas as holistic health, dreams, family life, finding your best vocation, reincarnation, ESP, meditation, personal spirituality, and soul growth in small-group settings. Call us today on our toll-free number:

1-800-333-4499
or
Explore our electronic visitors center on the Internet:
http://www.edgarcayce.org.
We'll be happy to tell you more about how
the work of the A.R.E. can help you!